Talent Management
A Step-by-Step Action-Oriented Guide Based on Best Practice

William J. Rothwell, Ph.D., SPHR
and
Maureen C. Jones
Maria T. Kirby
and
Frederick D. Loomis, Ph.D.

HRD Press, Inc. ❖ Amherst, Massachusetts

Published by: HRD Press, Inc.
22 Amherst Road
Amherst, MA 01002
1-800-822-2801 (U.S. and Canada)
413-253-3488
413-253-3490 (fax)
www.hrdpress.com

ISBN 978-1-59996-266-5

Production services by Jean Miller
Editorial services by Sally M. Farnham
Cover design by Eileen Klockars

Table of Contents

Preface

by *William J. Rothwell*

Talent Management (TM) is sometimes a term in search of meaning. It does not have one "right" meaning but can, instead, have many—depending on the problems that the Talent Management program is intended to solve and the organizational needs that the TM program is intended to meet.

This book opens with an Advance Organizer to help you zero in on what you need to know most. The book consists of ten chapters. Chapter 1 is entitled "Talent Management: The What, the Why, the How—and Problems to Avoid." It defines talent management and explains the business problems it is intended to solve. Chapter 2 reviews how to secure commitment for talent management from organizational leaders. It also emphasizes the importance of establishing measurable goals, clear roles and specific accountabilities. Chapter 3 examines job descriptions and competency models as the foundation for talent management. Chapter 4 explains the role of performance management in a talent management effort. Chapter 5 emphasizes the importance of forecasting future work and competencies. Chapter 6 summarizes subjective and objective ways of assessing potential (promotability). Chapter 7 describes how to identify and close developmental gaps. Chapter 8 reviews ways of meeting talent needs by recruiting internally and externally. Chapter 9 reviews ways to retain talented people, and Chapter 10 examines the topical issue of evaluating the success of a talent management program. An Appendix concludes the book, providing a tool for implementing the lessons found in the book.

Acknowledgments

William J. Rothwell would like to thank his wife, Marcelina, and his daughter Candice, for just being there for me. Although his son is stuck in the cornfields of Illinois, Froilan Perucho is not to be forgotten either for just being the wonderful person he is.

All the authors of this book would also like to express appreciation to Aileen Zabellero for her help in coordinating our work.

Advance Organizer

by *William J. Rothwell*

Complete the following Organizer before you read the book. Use it as a diagnostic tool to help you assess what you most want to know about talent management—and where you can find it in this book *fast*.

The Organizer

Directions: Read each item in the Organizer below. Circle T (True), N/A (Not Applicable), or F (False) in the left column opposite each item. Spend about 10 minutes on the Organizer. Be honest! Think of talent management as you would like it to be—not what some expert says it is. When you finish, score and interpret the results using the instructions appearing at the end of the Organizer. Then be prepared to share your responses with others in your organization as a starting point for conceptualizing talent management. If you would like to learn more about any of the items below, refer to the number in the right-hand column to find the chapter in this book in which the subject is discussed.

The Questions

Circle your response for each item below:

Do you believe Talent Management in this organization has already...	Chapter in Book
T N/A F 1. been based on specific organizational problems to be solved?	1
T N/A F 2. been given a clear, specific definition?	1
T N/A F 3. been seen as an important means to the end of enhancing the organization's competitive advantage?	1
T N/A F 4. been given *measurable* goals to be achieved?	2
T N/A F 5. been operationalized by ensuring that each key stakeholder group has a clear role description to follow?	2
T N/A F 6. established clear accountabilities for each stakeholder group to enact his or her role?	2
T N/A F 7. been based on up-to-date job descriptions?	2
T N/A F 8. been based on up-to-date competency models?	2
T N/A F 9. Integrated performance management with current job descriptions?	4
T N/A F 10. integrated performance management with current competency models?	4
T N/A F 11. encouraged a future orientation by forecasting the work to be performed in the future?	5

Do you believe Talent Management in this organization has already...	Chapter in Book
T N/A F 12. encouraged a future orientation by forecasting the people needed in the future through future-oriented competency models?	5
T N/A F 13. accommodated objective ways, going beyond manager-only assessment, of individual potential (promotability)?	6
T N/A F 14. included ways to close developmental gaps (and thereby develop individuals and groups) through planned methods such as Individual Development Plans (IDPs)?	7
T N/A F 15. included ways to meet talent management needs by effectively using *internal recruitment* methods such as job posting?	8
T N/A F 16. included ways to meet talent management needs by effectively using *external recruitment* methods such as electronic recruiting (e-recruiting)?	8
T N/A F 17. included ways to retain talented people?	9
T N/A F 18. included ways to evaluate the results of the talent management effort?	10
_____ Total	

Scoring and Interpreting the Organizer

Give yourself 1 point for each T and a 0 for each F or N/A listed above. Total the points from the T column and place the sum in the line opposite the word **Total** above. Then interpret your score as follows:

SCORE

POINTS	INTERPRETATION
Above 17	Your organization may already have an effective talent management program. While improvements can be made, your organization has already matched many best practice talent management principles.
14 – 17	Improvements could be made in your organization's talent management practices. On the whole, however, your organization is already on the right track.
11 – 13	Your organization's talent management perceptions are not good. Read the book and plan to make significant improvements.
Below 11	Your organization is far away from effective talent management.

Chapter 1

Talent Management: The What, the Why, the How—and Problems to Avoid

by *William J. Rothwell*

This chapter introduces talent management. This chapter:

- defines the term *talent management* (TM),

- explains why talent management has commanded such attention in recent years,

- provides a step-by-step strategic model to guide implementation of a talent management program, and

- describes what typical problems should be avoided in implementing a talent management program.

What does talent management mean?

Talent management can be understood in more than one way. In one sense it could mean the same thing as succession planning, human capital management, or workforce planning; in another sense, it can be regarded as completely different. One common definition suggests that *talent management means the process of attracting, developing and retaining the best people*. Another common definition adds two more elements to the previous definition—that is, *deploying the best people* (which means making sure that the right people are in the right places) and *transferring the knowledge of the best people* (which means communicating lessons learned from experience with the business and its customers from those with more to those with less experience). In all these definitions, the operative and key word is "best." Let it be emphasized that "best" does not mean "who managers like the most," but rather "who performs their current jobs best and who is also promotable."

While definitions of talent management may vary, one thing is certain. However talent management is defined in an organization—and more than one definition is clearly possible—it should be tied directly to solving the business problems and meeting the challenges of the organization in which it is carried out. If it does that, it is likely to be successful. But if it is pursued as just another flavor of the month, it is doomed to fail.

Use the Worksheet in Exhibit 1-1 below to define what you and your organization mean by talent management.

Exhibit 1-1: A Worksheet to Define Talent Management

Directions: Use this worksheet to guide your thinking in preparing a clear, well-understood definition for talent management for your organization. Ask major stakeholders to define what they believe talent management is and what problems it can help to solve for the organization. Then feed back their efforts and reach agreement on the definition.
How is talent management defined in this organization?

Why is talent management commanding such attention?

There are several reasons why talent management has galvanized the attention of business leaders in recent years. This section reviews those reasons.

Reason 1: The global workforce is aging. Almost everyone knows that the world's population is aging. Declining birth-rates worldwide, coupled with increasing longevity in developed economies, means that there are simply fewer young people to recruit for entry level positions. While retirement ages vary around the world, one fact is clear: one million people worldwide cross the 60 year age mark every month, according to the 2002 Second World Assembly on Aging. In developed economies, women live longer than men; in developing economies, the reverse is true.

Economists sometimes point to the inescapable relationship between growing populations and growing economies. When a nation's population is increasing, its economic climate is improving. One important reason is that younger people spend more money than older people do. Conversely, when a nation's population is declining, its economic climate is eroding. Small wonder that the world's economic climate does not look so good in the parts of the world where the population is aging most—Greece, Spain, Italy, the UK, and even the U.S.

Consider that population aging has coincided with widespread corporate downsizing. While that was often done to drive down costs, a side effect is that there are fewer experienced workers to go around. One result is increased competition for a dwindling supply of veteran middle managers who are prepared to take the place of retiring senior managers. At the same time competition is also increasing for veteran front-line supervisors who are promotable to middle management. In the future, perhaps one way to address talent shortages is to revise definitions of what "retirement" means (see Rothwell, Sterns, Spokus, and Reaser, 2008).

Reason 2: Organizations need to improve productivity to achieve and sustain competitive advantage. One reason for globalization is the advent of technology that makes it easier to travel globally, communicate globally, and shift work globally. High wage nations in Western Europe and the U.S. must compete with work products from lower wage nations in Asia and, increasingly, in Africa. To achieve and sustain competitive advantage, Western firms must increase the productivity of their higher-wage workers to get more outputs to counteract higher labor and employee benefit costs. They do that through a range of methods that include process improvement, lean manufacturing, six sigma quality efforts, and many others. Talent management is one method by which to ensure that the work is done by the most productive people so as to get the best results.

Reason 3: Talent is mobile. Talented people do not need to stay in their home countries if they can move geographically and command higher wages and better benefits. To offset declining birth rates, some countries are encouraging immigration of skilled workers. Only five countries in the world actively seek immigrants: The United States, Israel, Canada, New Zealand, and Australia. Population growth in these nations is due almost entirely to immigration. Many nations now actively encourage immigration of skilled workers and entrepreneurs to fill jobs that cannot be readily recruited locally. Notable examples include Germany and Singapore due to recognition that the labor force is declining as the population ages. With the advent of the integration of the European Union and (in time) ASEAN nations, labor force mobility will grow. That will create growing need for, and interest in, talent management.

Reason 4: Talent is the only truly renewable resource. Modern economies are based on knowledge and on innovation. While land, capital and information technology can be purchased, human talent is the active ingredient in using knowledge and prompting innovation. It is human talent that founds businesses, finds new markets to serve, and comes up with new products and services to create competitive advantage. Investments in human capital pay off in economic growth for nations and for organizations. Talent management is a means by which to focus unified attention on the human side of the business.

A Step-by-Step Strategic Model to Guide Implementation of a Talent Management Program

Two kinds of models can be helpful when implementing a talent management program. A *strategic model* guides, and integrates, everything that the organization does over time to attract, develop and retain the best people. A *tactical model* guides what managers and workers should do every day to attract, develop and retain talent. A strategic model helps organizational leaders to integrate the talent management program to the organization and with each component of the program. A tactical model can help managers, and individuals, apply the strategic model in daily practice. Without a strategic model, it may not be clear how all parts of a talent management program relate to each other and to achieving the organization's strategic objectives. Without a tactical model, it may be difficult to execute the strategic model.

The key steps in a strategic model appear in Exhibit 1-2. The steps are described below. Subsequent chapters in this book drill down into more detail for each step of the model. While this book emphasizes the strategic view, it should be noted that the tactical side of talent management—that is, what each manager does to build talent—is also critically important (see Rothwell, 2009).

Exhibit 1-2: A Strategic Model for Talent Management: A Step-By-Step Approach

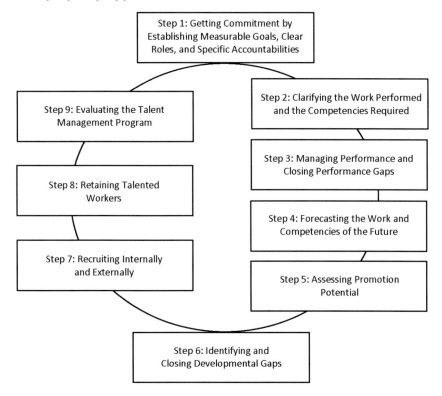

Step 1: Getting commitment and establishing measurable goals, clear roles, and specific accountabilities. The first, and perhaps the most important, step is to answer these questions:

- Why does the talent management program exist?

- What organizational needs will the program meet?

- What measurable results are sought from the program?

- Who are the key stakeholders for the talent management program, and what should each stakeholder's role be?

- How will each stakeholder group be held accountable for carrying out their roles and helping the organization achieve its measurable talent management program goals?

If it is helpful, use the worksheet in Exhibit 1-3 to guide your thinking and that of other decision-makers in the organization.

Exhibit 1-3: A Worksheet to Guide Clarification of Measurable Goals, Roles and Accountabilities for a Talent Management Program

Directions: Use this worksheet to guide your thinking in clarifying the measurable goals, roles and accountabilities for a talent management program. Ask the key stakeholders and decision-makers in the organization the questions in the left column below. Take notes in the right column. When you are finished, feed the results of individual interviews back to the stakeholders in a group and then facilitate their discussion to reach agreement on how to answer the questions.

Questions	Answers
1 Why does the talent management program exist?	
2 What organizational needs will the program meet?	
3 What measurable results are sought from the program?	
4 Who are the key stakeholders for the talent management program, and what should each stakeholder's role be?	
5 How will each stakeholder group be held accountable for carrying out their roles and helping the organization achieve its measurable talent management program goals?	

Step 2: Clarifying the work performed and the competencies required. To attract, develop and retain the best people, organizational leaders must have a clear and objective way of determining exactly who is the best. For that reason, organizations should have up-to-date job descriptions to clarify what work is done and competency models for each hierarchical level to clarify what kind of person gets the best results.

Consider:

- Does the organization have up-to-date job descriptions for targeted groups of people (such as front-line supervisors, middle managers, and top managers)?

- Does the organization have up-to-date competency models for targeted groups of people?

If the answer to one or both questions is "no," then an important step is to secure updated job descriptions and competency models. (For ideas about how to build competency models, see Dubois & Rothwell, 2000.)

Step 3: Managing performance and closing performance gaps. *Performance management* is another commonly used term in human resource management. And, like so many other terms, it actually has more than one meaning. But, in common language, it usually means efforts to plan, monitor and evaluate how well people are carrying out their job responsibilities and are demonstrating the competencies associated with successful or outstanding work performance.

In recent years, many organizational leaders have tried to use a balanced scorecard to describe what successful organizational performance should look like. What are the organization's strategic objectives for financial, customer, business process and learning and growth? Those objectives are then cascaded down the organization by functional area and even by job category. Not all work activities or results are equally important; not all behaviors are equally important. Some are more important than others. The most important desired work results for a division, department or individual are key performance indicators. They are linked on the one hand to the balanced scorecard and on the other hand to the behaviors linked to successful competencies.

Leaders can pinpoint performance gaps by comparing individual performance to key performance indicators and to desired behaviors. Closing performance gaps means narrowing (or eliminating) differences between ideal and actual performance. There are many ways to do that. Some of the ways involve helping individuals do their jobs better by equipping them with the knowledge, skills and attitudes they need to get results. Other ways may involve changing job duties, tools, equipment, or other resources given to individuals to do their jobs.

Step 4: Forecasting the work and competencies of the future.
Times change. Business conditions change. Work activities and competencies may thus change over time.

As a direct result of external environmental change, leaders must find ways to forecast what changes will occur in the work over time and what changes will occur in the competencies necessary for job success over time.

Furthermore, it takes time to develop people. Preparation for the next higher level of responsibility does not occur overnight. For that reason, a forecast is needed to clarify what kind of work and people are needed to realize the organization's strategic goals.

Step 5: Assessing promotion potential. If one goal of talent management is to help individuals realize their potential, it just makes sense to be clear what the term *potential* actually means. Performance is typically equated with *present job success;* potential is typically equated with *expected or likely future job success at higher levels of responsibility.* Understood in that sense, then, potential means "promotability."

Performance management is relatively straightforward. It addresses the simple question "how well are people achieving targeted work results and demonstrating behaviors linked to productivity"? But potential assessment is not so straightforward because it is difficult to determine how well individuals could perform if they were promoted. Potential assessment thus addresses the question "how well are people likely to achieve desired work results and demonstrate behaviors linked to productivity if they are promoted in the future to a higher level of responsibility"?

Step 6: Identifying and closing developmental gaps. The difference between ideal and actual work performance and behaviors is called a *performance gap*. But the difference between how well an individual is likely to perform at a higher level of responsibility and how well he or she presently performs is a *development gap*. When performance gaps are closed, individuals perform their jobs effectively. But when development gaps are closed, individuals are ready for promotion because they match the competency profile of the ideal performer at a higher level of responsibility.

A *performance improvement plan* (PIP), usually part of performance management, is the action plan to close performance gaps. In contrast, an *individual development plan* (IDP) is the action plan that describes how to narrow or close development gaps. The two should be kept separate so as not to confuse managers or workers on what they represent.

There are many ways to close gaps. While sending people off to training may be the first thing that occurs to managers when they are asked to close gaps, the reality is that most performance improvement and most development occurs on the job. For that reason, it is important to identify what people, work activities, and places will help individuals build their competencies and thereby close their gaps. (See Rothwell & Kazanas, 1999.)

Step 7: Recruiting internally and externally. There are only two ways to acquire talent. One way is to develop it internally. The other way is to recruit it internally (from inside the organization) or externally (from outside the organization). Recruitment must therefore be integrated with development. Talent acquisition and talent development should thus be regarded on the same basis, using competencies—as made measurable by behavioral indicators or work outputs—as the common denominator.

Internal recruitment is often handled through manager nominations and job posting. But many job posting systems, rooted in outmoded seniority-based thinking, cry out for retooling. Worse, in downsized organizations, managers often do not wish to grant approval to their best people to post for open positions—even when those may result in promotions. The reasons are simple. Managers worry that they will not be able to replace those they lose or will not be able to replace them with workers of comparable ability.

Recruitment should be competency-based—as should other elements of HR (see Dubois & Rothwell, 2004). Essential to external recruitment is the organization's employee brand, not to be confused with the organization's brand name. The *employee brand* is the organization's reputation as an employer. Employer brands answer the question "why are people attracted to apply to some organizations, and why do they stay?"

Step 8: Retaining talented workers. When an organization's leaders have invested substantial resources in a talent management program, they will just naturally want to keep the people they have invested in attracting or developing. Most organization have robust recruitment or development programs. But far fewer have robust retention programs. (See Rothwell, 2007).

Consider whether the organization has:

- Established measurable goals for a retention program that clarify how retention will meet organizational needs

- Clarified the roles to be played by key stakeholders in retaining talent

- Established accountability systems to make sure stakeholders play their parts in achieving measurable retention goals

- Targeted which individuals or types of individuals are most important for retention

- Identified methods to retain talent

- Implemented the methods to retain talent

- Measured how well the methods work in retaining talent

- Periodically evaluated how well the organization is retaining targeted talent

One way to ensure that talent management is effective is to emphasize how it can benefits individuals. For that reason, it may be helpful to launch a career planning program and integrate it with the organization's succession or talent management program (see Rothwell, Jackson, Knight, Lindholm, with Wang & Payne, 2005).

Step 9: Evaluating the talent management program. Evaluation is the final step in a talent management program. That is not to say that no evaluation occurs until all other steps are carried out. Instead, it means that the talent management program should be periodically monitored. If the talent management program was established with measurable goals that are tied to achieving the organization's strategic objectives, then it should be relatively easy to monitor goal achievement during implementation and periodically (such as at the end of each year).

Talent management professionals should not assume that all talent management programs should be assessed for cost/benefit or return on investment. While that is always an option, the real question is *"what information do decision-makers wish to be given periodically to ensure that the talent management program is contributing to organizational goals"*?

Common metrics used to evaluate talent management include:

- What percentage of people are promoted internally versus hired externally?

- How long does it take to fill key positions?

- What ratings (performance reviews) are given to those who are promoted from within over their first years following promotion?

- What is the turnover rate of high potentials, and how does that turnover rate compare to that for average performers?
- What percentage of each job category are considered high potentials, and what percentage is a desired target?
- What percentage of individual development plans (IDPs) are successfully completed on an annual basis?

These metrics are, of course, not the only ones that may be used. The key is to measure against the goals established for the program.

Typical Problems to Avoid When Implementing a Talent Management Program

There are several typical problems that should be avoided as a talent management program is formulated and implemented. It is worth reviewing the problems—and what can be done to avoid or minimize them.

A first problem: talent management is sometimes considered to be a human resources program only. That is a formula for failure. The reason: the HR department cannot hold senior executives accountable for carrying out their roles in achieving measurable talent development goals. Only the Board of Directors and the CEO can do that. A talent management program must be led by senior leaders and not by HR. HR does have a role—but it is not as process owner. That role belongs to the CEO and should not be delegated.

A second problem: about 70 percent of all talent management programs fail within the first 3 years. And it is easy to understand why. Managers undertake a talent management program to solve a noticeable problem such as a high number of pending retirements or too few well-qualified people to meet organizational needs. When the program actually works, managers lose interest—and then the program fails.

To avoid this problem—which could be regarded as failure stemming from program success—organizational leaders should annually review the measurable goals guiding the talent management program. If they do that, they can recalibrate the goals on an annual basis. The result: the talent management program will always be attuned to meeting continuing business needs.

A third problem: organizational leaders have unrealistic expectations about how quickly they can roll out a comprehensive, state-of-the-art talent management program. It is simply not possible to change corporate culture with a snap of the fingers. If the organization does not have a culture that supports objective decision-making about people, then it will take time to establish and implement competency models. (It is possible to get a Harvard MBA and never hear a word about competency models.)

To avoid this problem, decision-makers should think about implementation of talent management in phases. They should be very clear what results they want from the talent program and from each phase of implementing it. And they should make sure they are clear about measurable goals, the roles of key stakeholders, and accountability systems. If change is planned, then it can be implemented successfully. But the key is to *plan* it.

Chapter Summary

This chapter introduced talent management. It defined talent management, explained why talent management has commanded such attention in recent years, and provided a step-by-step strategic model to guide implementation of a talent management program. Finally, it described what typical problems should be avoided in implementing a talent management program.

The next chapter examines ways to get commitment for the talent management program. It also describes how to establish measurable talent management goals, clarify roles of key stakeholder groups, and establishing specific accountabilities for each stakeholder group.

Chapter 2

Step 1: Getting Commitment and Establishing Measurable Goals, Clear Roles, and Specific Accountabilities

by *William J. Rothwell*

The first step in Talent Management is getting commitment—that is, showing organizational decision-makers why a talent management program is warranted and why it deserves time, money, staff, and attention (see Exhibit 2-1 on the following page). This chapter thus focuses on the first step. Once commitment is secured, it is then necessary to clarify exactly what goals should be achieved from the Talent Management program to meet organizational needs, secure agreement among decision-makers on those goals, clarify what roles are to be carried out by various stakeholder groups in the Talent Management effort, and establish specific accountabilities for enacting the roles and helping the organization achieve its measurable Talent Management goals. This chapter focuses on each of these topics.

Getting Commitment

How can decision-makers be convinced that there is need to act on Talent Management? That is a question pondered by many HR professionals, who often complain that it is tough to secure and sustain necessary top management commitment (Rothwell & Kazanas, 2003).

Exhibit 2-1: The Step-by-Step Talent Management Model—Step 1

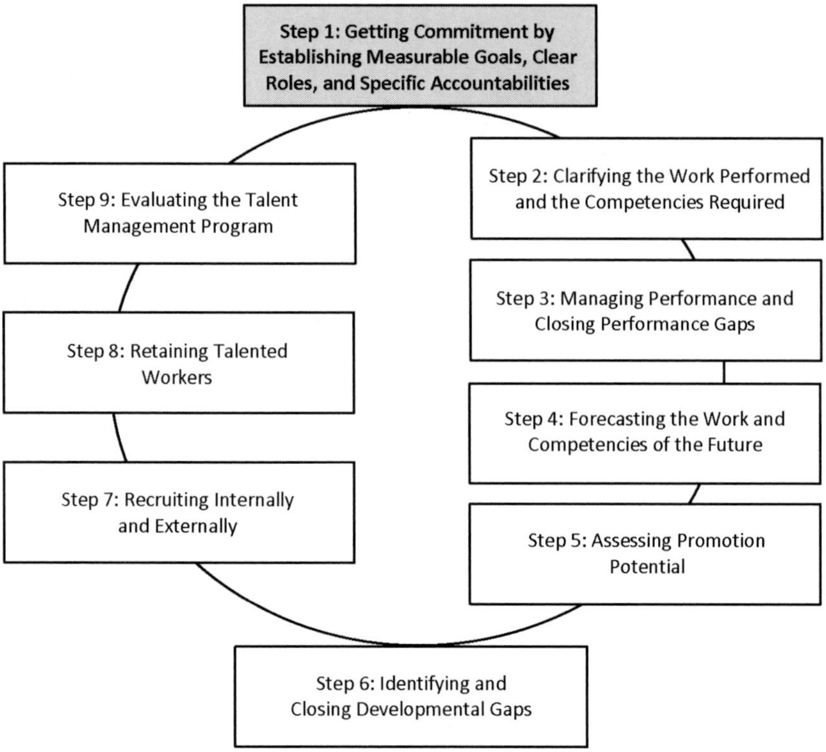

Commitment is not "on" or "off," like a light switch. It is more like a rheostat, a switch with infinite gradations. It is important as a starting point to clarify what commitment is desired from each affected stakeholder group. What time, money, staff and other resources—such as decision-maker time and active participation—is essential for the talent management program to be successful? Answering that question can be useful to become clear what behaviors are essential.

There are three common scenarios that a talent management initiator may face. The first is that decision-makers see little or no need; the second is that only some decision-makers see the need for a program; and the third is many decision-makers agree on the need for action. A different strategy is important, depending on the scenario.

Scenario 1: Decision-makers see little or no need. In Scenario 1, decision-makers do not see the need for talent management. To be sure, they may pay it lip service. But they are not really committed. They believe other issues are of more strategic importance.

If this is the situation in which you find yourself, then you must find out what the leaders and decision-makers do care about. Then you must craft the talent management effort as a means to the end of solving important problems that the decision-makers do see. To find out what the decision-makers care about, ask them. Conduct interviews with those you can get in to see. Ask them questions like these:

- What do you believe are some of the biggest challenges this organization faces?

- What are the biggest challenges in achieving our strategic goals?

- How do you believe HR efforts could best contribute to achieving success in addressing the problems or challenges the organization faces now and may face in the future?

Use the Worksheet in Exhibit 2-2 on the following page to help you collect this information.

Exhibit 2-2: An Interview Guide to Discover Key Issues in Talent Management

Directions: Use this interview guide to discover key issues in talent management. Pose the questions in the left column below to key decision-makers in your organization. Take notes in the right column. When you are finished with all interviews, look for common patterns of agreement and disagreement and feed the results back to the decision-makers.	
Questions for Decision-Makers	**Notes About Answers**
1. What do you believe are some of the biggest challenges this organization faces?	
2. What are the biggest challenges in achieving our strategic goals?	
3. How do you believe HR efforts could best contribute to achieving success in addressing the problems or challenges the organization faces now and may face in the future?	

Use the results of the interviews as a starting point to clarify the goals of a talent management program. Feed the common themes across the interviews, as well as major points of disagreement, back to the organization's leaders. Use that information to gain some agreement on what results the talent management should achieve.

Scenario 2: Some decision-makers see the need. If only some decision-makers see the need for a talent management program, then find out why they regard it as so important. Craft a short white paper that summarizes their positions. Let them review it and critique it. Then share it with the decision-makers who are less convinced. The goal is to get the organizational leaders aligned in their sense of urgency for the program.

Scenario 3: Many decision-makers see the need. This scenario is the best one to confront. It is highly desirable. But it does have a disadvantage. If all decision-makers are unified in their view of how important talent management is, they may also develop unrealistic expectations about how quickly such a program can be designed, developed, and implemented. They may also not share exactly the same sense of priorities about what should be emphasized.

To help sort this out, you should ask decision-makers questions such as these:

- Why do you believe talent management is so important?

- How does talent management best contribute to meeting the business needs and strategic goals of the organization?

- Since talent management cannot be all things to all people, what do you believe are the most important goals to be achieved in the short term (say 1-2 years) and in the long term (say 3-5 years)? Why do you believe they are so important?

Use the Worksheet in Exhibit 2-3 on the following page to help you collect this information.

Exhibit 2-3: A Second Interview Guide to Discover Key Issues in Talent Management

> **Directions:** Use this interview guide to discover key issues in talent management. Pose the questions in the left column below to key decision-makers in your organization. Take notes in the right column. When you are finished with all interviews, look for common patterns of agreement and disagreement and feed the results back to the decision-makers.

Questions for Decision-Makers	Notes About Answers
1. Why do you believe talent management is so important?	
2. How does talent management best contribute to meeting the business needs and strategic goals of the organization?	
3. Since talent management cannot be all things to all people, what do you believe are the most important goals to be achieved in the short term (say 1–2 years) and in the long term (say 3–5 years)? Why do you believe they are so important?	

Establishing Measurable Goals

Why is the organization undertaking the talent management program? The answer to that question, when made measurable and when agreed on by all or most key decision-makers, is critical. The reason: the talent management program should be shaped to achieve these measurable goals.

Business experts differ in what they call objectives and goals. According to one view, an objective is desirable but is not measurable. A goal, on the other hand, is measurable. For instance, "hiring more people" is an objective, but "hiring 3 new managers" is a goal.

While setting measurable goals for a business effort might seem like an exercise from a first course in management, a basic practice for any business situation, it is often amazing how seldom those goals are clarified and made measurable for talent programs. Arguably, that may be one reason why about 70 percent of all talent management programs fail within the first 3 years.

There should be a logical and obvious connection between the business problem that the talent management program is intended to solve and the measurable goals to be achieved. As noted in the previous chapter, most talent programs are undertaken in Western countries to address a tidal wave of expected retirements stemming from Baby Boomers exiting from the workplace or in Eastern countries to find the talented people to sustain explosive business growth.

If the problem centers on pending retirements, then it just makes sense to estimate how many such retirements to expect and over what time horizon. That can be done by starting with payroll records. Most organizations capture date of birth as an essential data element in payroll records. A simple computerized report can be conducted to estimate how many people will reach retirement age in each year. While not everyone who is eligible to retire will do so—unless legally-mandated by national laws to do so (which vary globally)—the goal of conducting such a study, called a *retirement risk assessment*, is to estimate what percentage of an organization's workforce is retirement eligible in a given year. That can be done for the entire organization. Then more detailed reports can be run to identify estimated retirement eligibility by level of the organization, by job code, by division or department, and by geographical area.

The aim of this effort is to pinpoint the locations where the risk of retirement eligibility is highest. I believe that the best way to do that is to look at the data in rolling 3-year periods—such as years 2012, 2013 and 2014 or years 2013, 2014 and 2015—to pick up trends and find out over rolling three year timespans what specific job codes, departments, divisions, or locations will face the highest risk of possible retirements. That will provide convincing evidence for decision-makers about the problem to be solved.

If the problem centers around the need for talent to help the organization expand—a common problem in explosive growth economies such as China, Vietnam, Malaysia or Thailand—then it just makes sense to estimate how many and what kind of people will be needed over time to sustain forecasted business growth. For instance, if a retailer plans to open 5 stores per year, it is easily estimated that sufficient talent must be recruited or developed and promoted to fill that number of positions. Of course, allowances must be made for turnover of existing staff and for turnover of those hired or promoted.

My research has shown that Talent Management programs can meet many possible goals. But they cannot meet all goals equally well. Someone must set priorities and focus them so that the talent management programs achieves the desired results.

Additional *objectives* might include:

- Increasing diversity of various groups (such as women) at different levels of the organization

- Demonstrating social responsibility by employing members of the communities served by the organization (rather than importing expatriates from other locales)

- Providing work challenges for talented people so that they will not quit

- Engaging older workers so that they will stay

- Preparing talented people for higher level responsibility

- Transferring specialized knowledge of customers, products, or work processes gained from experience from more to less experienced workers

- Transferring specialized business contacts from those who enjoy those relationships with customers, vendors, suppliers, distributors, competitors, industry partners, or other key people to those who do not enjoy the same social contacts

An important aim is to set priorities and transform immeasurable objectives into measurable goals to guide the Talent Management program. Only in that way can resources be targeted with greatest economy.

An additional challenge is to get most key decision-makers to agree to, and commit to achieving, the goals. That can be more difficult than it might sound. One reason is that each senior manager actually wears two hats: one as part of the executive group governing the whole business and a second hat as leader of his or her own group within the organization. The temptation is for leaders to think of only one hat—usually the unique needs of the group for which they are chiefly responsible. But effective Talent Management should also consider the needs of the entire organization, and the goals should be calibrated for achieving those results.

Use the worksheet in Exhibit 2-4 on the following page to help decision-makers clarify their objectives for the talent management program and turn them into measurable goals.

Exhibit 2-4: A Worksheet to Define Talent Management Objectives and Goals

Directions: Use this worksheet to help decision-makers clarify their desired results from a talent management program. Ask major stakeholders to describe what results they would like to see from the talent management program and then ask them to describe how those results might be measured. Feed back what they say and try to get them to reach agreement on measurable targets for the talent management program.

What results should a talent management program attain? How can those results be measured?

Additional metrics can be established. For instance, the organization's leaders can set a target for a percentage of internal promotions and external hires. The appropriate metric may depend on the competitive nature of the organization's industry. In government, a rule of thumb is 80 percent to be promoted from within and 20 percent to be hired from outside. In a high-tech manufacturing, a different rule of thumb might apply—such as 20 percent promoted from within and 80 percent hired from outside.

Another metric that may be used is the time to fill metric. How long does it take to fill positions? If the organization has an effective talent management program, that time to fill should decline because suitable internal candidates are continuously groomed for promotion and external candidates are assembled on short lists in anticipation of possible vacancies.

Establishing Clear Roles for Each Stakeholder Group

Who are the stakeholders who are influenced by the Talent Management program? The key stakeholders should be clarified and their roles made clear so that they can be held accountable for "doing what they should do" to make the Talent Management program work.

Typical stakeholders (and this list is not intended to be exhaustive) might include:

- Stockholders (for publicly-traded companies)
- Board of Director members
- Executives
- Middle managers
- Front-line supervisors
- Unions
- The HR department
- Workers

Each stakeholder should be clear on what he or she—or the group—should do and what others should do. Otherwise, at the end of the year, everyone will engage in finger pointing about who did not do what they were supposed to do. Of course, if roles are not clarified at the start, some will not carry out a role that should rightfully be theirs. One danger: everyone expects HR to do everything. And this is neither practical nor desirable. Making that mistake leads to guaranteed failure. The reason: HR cannot hold senior executives accountable because only the CEO and the Board can do that.

Use the worksheet in Exhibit 2-5 on the following page to clarify the roles of different stakeholder groups. It makes sense to involve those stakeholders in coming up with their own role descriptions of what they should do to make the Talent Management program successful.

Exhibit 2-5: A Worksheet to Clarify the Role of Various Groups in Talent Management

Directions: Use this worksheet to help decision-makers clarify what roles should be played by various stakeholder groups in implementing the talent management program. For each group listed below, ask decision-makers what parts that group should play in helping the organization achieve its talent management goals.

Stakeholder Group	What should members of this group do?
Stockholders (for publicly-traded companies)	
Board of Director members	
Executives	
Middle managers	
Front-line supervisors	
Unions	
The HR department	
Employees/workers	

Holding Stakeholders Accountable

Many talent management programs fail because there are no consequences for decision-makers if they perform and no consequences if they fail to perform. You get what you pay for. And you get what you measure and hold people accountable for. And so accountability systems for talent management are critical.

There are different ways to hold people accountable. One way is to place an executive bonus plan, when it exists, at risk for meeting measurable talent management goals for each senior executive. One approach: hold 80 percent of the executive bonus plan at risk for meeting measurable, annual goals for production, sales or other relevant organizational targets and hold the other 20 percent at risk for meeting measurable, annual goals for talent management. Of course, coming up with the metrics to measure achievement should relate to the business goals. (For instance, if the goal is to prepare people to address pending retirements, each division can be given a target of a number of people to be prepared. Those can be measured using objective assessments as outlined in the chapter on assessing potential.)

In organizations that do not have executive bonus plans, there are alternative approaches to accountability. One idea is to build self-development and staff development into each manager's key performance indicators (KPIs), which are used in performance management. Another idea is to make it a policy that managers can only be promoted if they have prepared more than one possible successor for themselves.

There is no one right way. The approach to use depends on business needs. But ultimately decision-makers must come up with some kind of accountability system. If they do not, the talent management program will likely fail.

Chapter Summary

This chapter addressed four key questions. In establishing a talent management program, an organization's leaders should consider:

- How can the organization ensure commitment of its managers to the talent management program?

- What are the measurable goals to guide the talent management program, and how will their achievement meet business needs and solve business problems?

- Who are the stakeholders for the talent management program, and how can their respective roles be made clear for program implementation?

- How can stakeholders be held accountable for enacting their roles to help the organization meet measurable talent management goals?

Chapter 3

Step 2: Clarifying the Work Performed and the Competencies Required

by *William J. Rothwell*

It is not possible to develop or source talent without knowing how talent is specifically defined. In short, "you can't get what you want if you don't know what that is." To develop or source talent, decision-makers must know what people do, what results they achieve, and what people are most productive. For that reason, the second step in talent management is "clarifying the work performed" and "clarifying the competencies required" (see Exhibit 3-1 on the following page). The first has to do with work analysis and its product the job description, and the second has to do with competency identification and its product the competency model.

This chapter focuses on this second step of talent management. What is work analysis, and how is it carried out? What are the traditional problems with job descriptions, and how can they be improved? What is competency identification, and how is it carried out? What are some traditional problems with competency models, and how can they be solved? This chapter answers these important questions.

Exhibit 3-1: The Step-by-Step Talent Management Model—Step 2

```
                  ┌─────────────────────────────────┐
                  │  Step 1: Getting Commitment by   │
                  │ Establishing Measurable Goals,   │
                  │ Clear Roles, and Specific        │
                  │ Accountabilities                 │
                  └─────────────────────────────────┘

┌──────────────────────────┐     ┌──────────────────────────────┐
│ Step 9: Evaluating the   │     │ Step 2: Clarifying the Work  │
│ Talent Management Program│     │ Performed and the            │
└──────────────────────────┘     │ Competencies Required        │
                                 └──────────────────────────────┘

                                 ┌──────────────────────────────┐
┌──────────────────────────┐     │ Step 3: Managing Performance │
│ Step 8: Retaining        │     │ and Closing Performance Gaps │
│ Talented Workers         │     └──────────────────────────────┘
└──────────────────────────┘
                                 ┌──────────────────────────────┐
                                 │ Step 4: Forecasting the Work │
┌──────────────────────────┐     │ and Competencies of the      │
│ Step 7: Recruiting       │     │ Future                       │
│ Internally and Externally│     └──────────────────────────────┘
└──────────────────────────┘
                                 ┌──────────────────────────────┐
                                 │ Step 5: Assessing Promotion  │
                                 │ Potential                    │
                                 └──────────────────────────────┘

              ┌──────────────────────────────┐
              │ Step 6: Identifying and      │
              │ Closing Developmental Gaps   │
              └──────────────────────────────┘
```

Defining Work Analysis and Describing How Work Analysis Is Carried Out

Work analysis is the process of determining how work is performed. It involves studying how work is done. A typical product of a work analysis is a job description that often lists at least:

- The job title
- The purpose of the job or work in a sentence or two
- Reporting relationships (to whom the job reports and who the job incumbent oversees)
- A representative list of work activities or work duties (what do people do in the job?)

- A list of minimum education, experience and other requirements essential to do the job (commonly called a *job specification*)

Use the Worksheet in Exhibit 3–2 to guide the preparation of a job description.

Exhibit 3-2: A Worksheet to Guide Preparation of a Job Description

Directions: Use this worksheet to guide the preparation of an effective job description. For each item shown in the left column below, provide an answer in the right column.

Typical Components of a Job Description	Your Answer for a Specific Job
The job title	
The purpose of the job or work (in a sentence or two)	
Reporting relationships (to whom the job reports and who the job incumbent oversees)	*Reports to:* *Position that reports to this job:*
A representative list of work activities or work duties (what do people do in the job?)	*List representative duties:*

Exhibit 3-2 (continued)

A list of minimum education, experience, and other requirements essential to do the job (commonly called a *job specification)*	*Education:* *Experience:* *Other requirements:*

Many approaches exist to conducting work analysis (see, for instance, Prien, Goodstein, Goodstein, & Gamble, 2009). These approaches range from the superficial to the rigorous. A superficial (but commonly-used) approach is to ask the manager to write the job description when a vacancy is to be filled. That is superficial because the manager is removed from the daily work and will typically write the description based on past job descriptions (which may be outdated) or inaccurate perceptions of how the work is done.

A more rigorous (and therefore more time-consuming and expensive) approach is for an HR representative to interview a job-holder and a direct supervisor of the job incumbent about the work performed. That is more rigorous because it captures more than one perspective. It thus permits double-checking on the responses of both job holders and their managers. Research indicates that supervisors and workers disagree on about 50 percent of the work activities and standards of performance. Without gaining the perspective of both job incumbent and supervisor, insights on the nature of these important differences in perspective are lost. That subsequently makes it less likely that the best candidate will be attracted or developed.

Many resources exist to make it easier to write job descriptions. For instance, online resources exist that consist of thousands of job descriptions. They can speed up the process, though (of course) it is always important to double-check the preferences about the work performed in the unique corporate culture of each organization. One example of a valuable resource is the database of BLR (see https://hr.blr.com/trial_v2/SignUp_Alt3.aspx?layoutID= 283&source=MKD&effort=1990) or the free resource of the U.S. government (see http://www.occupationalinfo.org/). Care must be taken in using these resources, however, since organizations—and their leaders—may differ in what they expect job holders to do or how they expect them to go about doing it.

Traditional Problems with Job Descriptions— and How to Solve Them

There are several traditional problems with job descriptions.

First, they are typically written with only a representative list of work activities or duties. They are thus not complete. A common approach is to list only *some* examples of the work performed and then add "and all other duties as assigned." The result: job descriptions can be misleading, or even inaccurate, because the duties listed may not be truly representative.

Second, they are focused on what people *do*—that is, work activities or duties—rather than the measurable results to be achieved. Work activities or duties, by themselves, are not measurable. What are the expected performance results of the job? What are the ideal or targeted performance results? How are results measured by output (work products) and by desired behaviors (what people do to achieve those results and carry out those activities)?

Third, job descriptions do not clearly indicate *criticality* (that is, importance to job success) or *frequency* (how often performed) are the work activities or duties. When reading a list of representative activities or duties, supervisors and job incumbents alike may be hard pressed to indicate what is really important.

There are several solutions to the problems mentioned above.

First, job descriptions may be based on a comprehensive list of the work activities or duties performed. Devising such a list can be done by observing the work and noting what job incumbents actually do as they work. Another approach is to bring together a group of experienced job incumbents and their supervisors and ask the question "what do you do on a daily basis?" The so-called DACUM method—where DACUM is an acronym standing for "developing a curriculum"—can be most useful in developing a comprehensive list of work activities that are actually performed. A DACUM chart (the product of a DACUM process) is essentially an extremely detailed job description that describes a robust, comprehensive list of what people do on their jobs. For more information on DACUM,

see http://www.dacumohiostate. com/DACUM%20Research%
20Chart%20Bank.pdf.

A DACUM chart is usually organized by categories (such as
paperwork) and then the activities associated with it (such as "fills
out performance reviews," "meets with customers," and so forth). A
completed DACUM chart is essentially a detailed roadmap of everything that people do on their jobs. It answers only one question:
"*What do people do on the job now?*" It does not answer additional
questions—such as "*what should people be doing on their jobs
now?*", "*what does management wish people were doing on their
jobs?*", or "*what should people be doing on their jobs to enhance
competitive advantage or best serve customers?*" Answering these
and other questions requires additional steps to drill down into
each activity to discover who does it, what they do exactly, how
they do it step-by-step in tasks, and what individual or personal
characteristics matter most to job success.

Second, there is no law or rule that requires that job descriptions
be activity-based. It is simply a convention. They could be written
in results-oriented terms, indicating average measurable performance targets to be achieved or desired performance targets.

In recent years, and with the advent of the Balanced Scorecard,
organizational leaders are requiring that performance management systems shore up and address the weaknesses inherent in job
descriptions. Performance management can do that by indicating
what work results are most important (key performance indicators) and what work behaviors are most important (the behaviors
associated with the organization's success).

Third, to address the problem that job descriptions do not
indicate what is really important, organizational leaders may take
several steps to address this problem. One is to indicate on the job
description the level of criticality to job success of the work activity
(as on a 5-point Likert-style scale) and/or the frequency that the
activity is to be performed on the job (such as many times daily,
sometimes, infrequently, and so forth). Another is to use the
performance management system to zero in on what is most
critical or most frequently performed in the work.

To prepare job descriptions effectively for talent management, take the following steps:

1. Identify the targeted job categories to be examined

2. Update the job descriptions and then focus them on desired work results and behaviors linked to those work results

3. Make sure that the updating process includes input from supervisor and one or more job incumbents

4. Establish a routine means by which to update all job descriptions on a continuing basis (such as by using the performance management system as a means by which to require regular updating of all job descriptions)

Describing Competency Identification and How It Is Carried Out

While a job description quite literally describes the work to be performed, a competency model describes—in narrative fashion—the kind of person who does that work successfully or outstandingly. To state it another way, a job description summarizes the work to be performed but a competency model describes the human being who does the work adequately or well. Unfortunately, some confusion still exists today about the meaning of competencies.

But one thing is clear. In modern economies, the key to competitive advantage is the talent that the individual worker brings to his or her job. Job descriptions were invented in the industrial age to describe what work people do. The abilities of individual workers were simply less important than the people who did the work. But in a knowledge economy, the abilities to interact with other people and to innovate become critical to competitive advantage. Competency models simply do better than job descriptions in clarifying the unique individual characteristics that lead to success with other people.

Competencies may be identified in several ways.

First, an organization's leaders may simply choose to go the low cost (and low rigor) approach of adopting a competency model without modification from some other sources. Type in "competency model" into a search engine, and thousands of competency models can be readily found. Another source is the competency clearinghouse of the U.S. Department of Labor (see www.careerone stop.org/CompetencyModel/).

Second, an organization's leaders may choose to go to the slighter more costly (and higher rigor) approach of modifying and adopting a competency model from some other sources. Select a model from a similar organization and then tailor it to meet the unique corporate cultural needs of one corporate culture. The typical steps in doing that are: (1) work with job incumbents and their immediate supervisors to develop a rough draft model of a competency model for a targeted group from some other source; (2) validate the model by surveying the entire population (or a statistically generalizable sample of the population) of job incumbents and their immediate supervisors; and (3) secure approval of leaders to implement the model in the organization.

Third, an organization's leaders may choose to go the most costly (but also most rigorous) approach of building a competency model from scratch to fit the unique corporate culture and strategic needs of the business. That is a time-consuming, labor-intensive and expensive option. But it is also likely to be most effective if used properly because it is uniquely fitted to the needs of the business.

Building a competency model from scratch requires time and effort. Typical steps include:

1. Identifying a targeted group of performers (such as top managers, middle managers or front-line supervisors)

2. Pinpointing the average and superior performers based on measurable work results or objectively-identifiable achievements

3. Conducting Behavioral Event Interviews (BEIs) with the average and superior performers to identify key characteristics of each group, shared characteristics across groups, and characteristics uniquely linked only to superior performers

4. Developing a rough draft list of competencies from shared themes across the interviews

5. Making the competencies measurable through behavioral indicators and/or measurable work outputs by competency

Subsequent steps after the fifth one listed above are identical to those in the modified approach. In other words, develop a rough draft model of a competency model for a targeted group from some other source. Then validate the model by surveying the entire population (or a statistically generalizable sample of the population) of job incumbents and their immediate supervisors. Finally, secure approval of leaders to implement the model in the organization by incorporating it into all or some facets in making employment decisions—such as recruiting, training, developing, coaching, appraising, and rewarding all workers.

For more information on competency modeling, see Dubois & Rothwell (2000) and Sanghi (2007).

Traditional Problems with Competency Models and How to Solve Them

Competency models do have advantages over job descriptions. Since they focus on people rather than work, they do not date as quickly. After all, competencies are in people, and people do not change that much. And competency models do a better job than job descriptions of capturing those tough-to-define soft skills such as emotional intelligence and interpersonal ability that are so critical to success in today's organizations.

But competencies also have disadvantages. They are worth mentioning.

First, few managers understand what they are. And even some HR professionals are challenged to know competency work. Consequently, adopting competency models requires a continuing communication process to explain, and show the value of, competencies. One management briefing or note to employees will not be sufficiently effective in making the case for change. And make no mistake: using competencies as a foundation for HR decisions is a major change effort.

Second, the term competency does not have a standardized definition. Nor do terms associated with it—such as behavioral indicators, work outputs, and so forth. Every consulting firm that works with competencies uses different language and terminology to describe the same concepts. That can lead to significant confusion.

To overcome both problems requires that an organization's leaders mount a continuing communication effort to explain and use competencies. It can be helpful to revisit the entire HR system—that is, all ways that the organization works with people—and find ways to embed competency models into every element. Only if people must use competencies in everything they do with people will they come to understand what they are. That may require systematically reinventing and transforming the entire HR system of the organization. Like any large-scale and long-term change effort, that can be prone to pitfalls and risks. But undertaking it is critical if descriptions of talent are to be made more objective and less prone to popularity contests.

Chapter Summary

This chapter examined work analysis and competency models. To recruit and develop talent in a talent management program, organizational leaders must have an objective sense of what talent is. Job descriptions and competency models can provide that sense.

This chapter defined work analysis explained how it is carried out, reviewed problems with traditional job descriptions and suggested ways to solve those problems. The chapter also defined competency models, explained how the process of developing such models is carried out, reviewed traditional problems with competency models and how to solve them.

The next chapter focuses on the third step in talent management, performance management.

Chapter 4

Step 3: Managing Performance and Closing Performance Gaps

by *William J. Rothwell*

Two principles are fundamental to talent management. The first is that promotions should not be given to people *failing* in their present jobs. The second is that promotions should not be given to people *just because they are good or excellent in their present jobs*. To avoid promoting those who are failing in their present jobs, it is essential to have an effective performance management system in the organization. Workers should be evaluated against the measurable performance targets (or key performance indicators) they are given. They should also be evaluated against the behaviors expected of competent workers at their level on the organization chart.

This chapter focuses on performance management. It is essential to talent management because managing talent requires careful attention to workers' present work performance as well as to their future potential (see Exhibit 4-1 on the following page). But just what is performance management? What role does it play in talent management? How is a performance management system integrated with the organization's talent management system? What should be done if an existing performance management system is not well integrated? What steps should be taken to ensure an effective performance management system is implemented and sustained in an organization? This chapter addresses these important questions.

Exhibit 4-1: The Step-by-Step Talent Management Model—Step 3

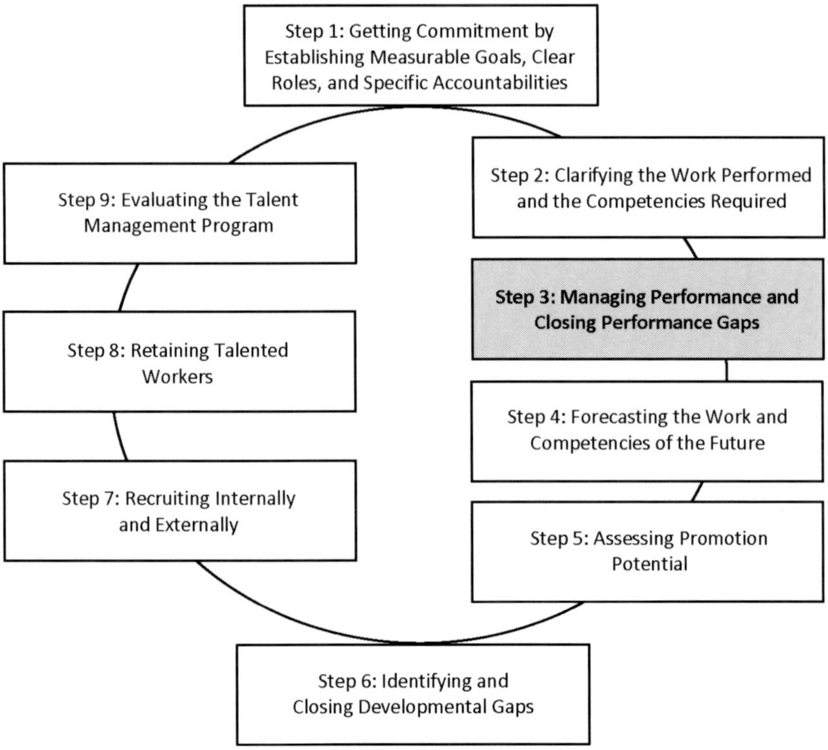

```
┌─────────────────────────────────┐
│   Step 1: Getting Commitment by  │
│  Establishing Measurable Goals,  │
│   Clear Roles, and Specific       │
│          Accountabilities         │
└─────────────────────────────────┘
```

Step 9: Evaluating the Talent Management Program

Step 2: Clarifying the Work Performed and the Competencies Required

Step 3: Managing Performance and Closing Performance Gaps

Step 8: Retaining Talented Workers

Step 4: Forecasting the Work and Competencies of the Future

Step 7: Recruiting Internally and Externally

Step 5: Assessing Promotion Potential

Step 6: Identifying and Closing Developmental Gaps

Defining Performance Management

Performance management can actually have many meanings, not just one.

In some organizations, performance management is just a new term for performance appraisal. Workers perform throughout an evaluation period—typically a year—and are then evaluated by their immediate supervisors. Such after-the-fact performance reviews can be prone to many problems, since workers are never sure what their work goals are or what behaviors they are expected to demonstrate. Often that is left up to managers to decide. Such approaches can be prone to subjective judgments that can be damaging to individual job satisfaction, work group morale, and even to job performance if supervisors are rating on factors other than objectively measurable work results and clearly-defined work behaviors.

Traditional performance management is undertaken for many reasons. It can provide workers with valuable feedback on their job performance, of course. It can also serve to:

- Assess training needs

- Justify pay raises

- Provide useful information in making promotion decisions

- Guide coaching efforts between worker and manager

- Document outstanding, average or below average performance

- Guide corrective action and document performance, behavioral or other problems

In traditional HR thinking, job descriptions establish clear responsibilities. Performance appraisal permits a check of how well the job incumbent is meeting these responsibilities over specific time periods, such as annually. That establishes performance appraisal as an accountability and management control system that permits a periodic quality control check on worker performance. For more on the topic, see Aquinis, 2008; Cokins, 2009; and Parmenter, 2010. Examples of performance appraisal/management forms may be found at http://www. halogensoftware.com/products/halogen-eappraisal/ employee- evaluation-forms/ and at http://www. humanresources. hrvinet.com/performance-appraisal-examples/.

Current approaches to performance management go beyond the simplistic notion of after-the-fact reviews of worker performance to include an entire cycle. First, the organization's leaders establish the strategic goals of the organization, perhaps using a robust approach such as the Balanced Scorecard. Strategic goals are cascaded down the organization by division, department, unit and worker. Each worker's goals are thus logically related to the organization's goals. They may take the form of Key Performance Indicators (KPIs), which encapsulate the critically-important results that the worker must deliver so that the organization will achieve its goals. Second, each worker and his or her manager plan performance targets for the review period. Third, worker performance is periodically reviewed—such as weekly, monthly, or quarterly—to determine how well the targets are being achieved. If problems exist, periodic reviews allow worker and manager to come together to review why those problems exist in performance and how they may be solved. Finally, at the end of the review period workers meet with their managers to review results and behaviors against the targets established at the beginning of the review cycle. At that time, future targets may also be planned so that the cycle may begin anew.

To develop Key Performance Indicators (KPIs), start by listing the organization's balanced scorecard goals. Then list the most important work activities/responsibilities for a job description. Indicate which work activities are most critical to achieving the organization's balanced scorecard goals. These become the KPIs. Then list the behaviors linked to the competencies appropriate to the job category. This list of KPIs and related behaviors should then be the foundation for the performance management system. Use the Worksheet in Exhibit 4-2 on the following pages to aid in this process.

Exhibit 4-2: A Worksheet for Developing Performance Management Criteria for a Targeted Job

Directions: Use this Worksheet to develop performance management criteria—both Key Performance Indicators (KPIs) and Behaviors—relevant to a job category. Answer the questions below and on the following pages to derive the performance management criteria for a targeted job category. Add more enumerated items as needed. Add paper if needed.

What are the organization's balanced scorecard criteria? List them below.

1) _____

_____

2) _____

_____

3) _____

_____

4) _____

_____

5) _____

_____

6) _____

_____

7) _____

_____

Exhibit 4-2 (continued)

What are the most important activities linked to the organization's balanced scorecard? (List them and indicate how they are
measured. The numbers should correspond with the numbered
balanced scorecard criteria above.)

1) _____

_____

_____

2) _____

_____

_____

3) _____

_____

_____

4) _____

_____

_____

5) _____

_____

_____

6) _____

_____

_____

7) _____

_____

_____

Exhibit 4-2 (continued)

What are the KPIs for the job? List them below for each of the numbered balanced scorecard criteria and work activity or work activities.

1) _____

_____

_____

2) _____

_____

_____

3) _____

_____

_____

4) _____

_____

_____

5) _____

_____

_____

6) _____

_____

_____

7) _____

_____

_____

Exhibit 4-2 (continued)

What behaviors, relevant to the KPIs, are contained in the competency model for the organizational level of the job? List them below as appropriate for each of the three items above.

1) _____

_____

_____

2) _____

_____

_____

3) _____

_____

_____

4) _____

_____

_____

5) _____

_____

_____

6) _____

_____

_____

7) _____

_____

_____

Exhibit 4-2 (concluded)

What are the behaviors most appropriately linked to the KPIs?
List them below. (Remember, each numbered item should
correspond to the numbered balanced scorecard criteria.)

1) _____

_____

_____

2) _____

_____

_____

3) _____

_____

_____

4) _____

_____

_____

5) _____

_____

_____

6) _____

_____

_____

7) _____

_____

_____

When viewed according to this current approach, performance management is logically related to goal theory. According to goal theory, workers are increasingly likely to achieve targets when they know clearly what is expected of them and have a chance to discuss those goals with their immediate supervisors. Any real or perceived barriers can then be discussed and strategies established to address them—or else the goals can be changed so that they are more realistic.

The Role of Performance Management in Talent Management

As noted at the opening of this chapter, performance management plays a fundamentally important role in talent management. It provides a continuing process by which to assess how well individuals are meeting their responsibilities. Without performance management that is objectively-based, there is a risk that those who are not performing successfully will be rewarded or even promoted based solely on how much they are liked by their supervisors. While having a supervisor who likes you is a good thing, it should not be the sole criterion on which rewards or promotions are made. A better approach is to assess how well people are achieving objectively measurable results. How much the manager likes someone may have little or nothing at all to do with achieving measurable work results.

But performance management is not sufficient, by itself, to determine potential for promotion. The reason is simple enough. Performance management focuses only on how well people do their current jobs, not how well they could do jobs at a higher or different responsibility level. While it may be true, as many psychologists believe, that past performance is the best indicator of future performance, it should also be noted that it is quite helpful to have a sense of how well people will perform in jobs they have never done before. Is the role of the CEO the same as that of senior executive in charge of a division? Of course not. And so why should anyone assume that success at the senior executive level is the only necessary determinant of success as a CEO? The same principle applies for considering anyone for a promotion. A separate, more objective assessment of potential should be made.

When individual performance does not match expectations, there is need to establish a performance improvement plan (PIP). Examples of such forms and the procedures to go with them can be found online at such locations as http://www.foley.com/files/ tbl_s88EventMaterials/FileUpload587/1040/SamplePerformance ImprovementPlan.pdf and at http://www.nps.gov/training/tel/ Guides/PIP_pg_2006Aug22.pdf.

An important point: individuals are usually not considered for promotion if they are not doing their present jobs well. At the same time, good job performance does not mean that an individual is automatically promotable because good performance at one level does not necessarily guarantee success at different, higher levels of responsibility.

Integrating Performance Management and Talent Management

Most organizations have a performance management system. Some organizations have talent management programs. But the existence of one or both does not mean that they are well-integrated.

The essential point to understand in integrating them is that the descriptions of desirable work, work results, competencies and behaviors are:

- Linked to the organization's strategic goals

- Based on rigorous descriptions of the work to be performed

- Based on measurable results and behaviors linked to competency models for the targeted level (such as supervisor, manager, or executive)

On the other hand, if separate and unrelated efforts are under-taken to establish the organization's strategic goals and the organization's performance management system, then it is likely that they are not integrated. One consequence will be that the organization's direction is not considered when assessing how well individuals perform their jobs. That will lead to an ineffective talent management program.

Redirecting Performance Management when Not Integrated with Talent Management

So what do you do if your performance management system was developed and implemented before your organization's talent management program was established? That is, after all, the most likely situation that will exist when there is a disconnect or lack of integration between performance management and talent management.

If this is the case confronting you and your organization, then you may wish to consider forming a team of managers to review the performance management system—policies, forms and directions—against the goals and requirements of the talent management program. It is wise to develop a separate performance management form by management level—that is, executive, manager and supervisor—so as to be able to use performance management as a way to assess a worker's performance against work activities (as described on job descriptions) and work outputs and behaviors (as described in competency models).

Consider whether it is possible to do a simple revision without needing to undertake a major update of the performance management system. While a major update may be advisable to position performance reviews best against work and worker requirements, it can be difficult and time-consuming to achieve because it will require a revision of all policies, forms and support systems (such as software). It may also necessitate retraining all managers about how to use the new performance review system. For that reason, it may be easier to add to the performance management system rather than to revamp it from scratch.

Steps in Implementing and Sustaining an Effective Performance Management System

What are the steps in implementing and sustaining an effective performance management system? To that end, follow these major steps:

1. Clarify the organization's strategic goals using an approach like the Balanced Scorecard,

2. Form a committee representing high-level decision-makers and other users of the performance management system.

3. Brief the committee members on current thinking about performance management (that is, the importance of linking the organization's strategic goals, as described in the Balanced Scorecard, with work responsibilities and worker competencies).

4. Review sample forms and procedures for performance management (many of which may be found through a simple web search).

5. Task the team members to decide what should be the goals of the performance management system, what policies and procedures should govern it, how a form can be constructed to measure what is most important in worker job performance and behaviors, and what software support in the Human Resource Information System (HRIS) may be necessary for the new system to capture worker performance information over time.

6. Decide, as part of step 5, whether there should be one form for the entire organization or many forms, depending on type of worker.

7. Develop an action plan to implement the performance management system, including how it will be rolled out, how any previous performance management system will be closed down, who should receive training on the new system, and how the training will be designed and delivered.

8. Establish a follow-up strategy to ensure that information about the new performance management system is communicated, its implementation is tracked against a timeline and against project milestones, and (at a later time) the program's implementation is evaluated for continuing improvement.

Chapter Summary

This chapter focused on performance management. The chapter addressed such important questions as these: (1) What is performance management? (2) What role does it play in talent management? (3) How is a performance management system integrated with the organization's talent management system? (4) What should be done if an existing performance management system is not well integrated? (5) What steps should be taken to ensure an effective performance management system is implemented and sustained in an organization?

The next chapter focuses on the fourth step in talent management. That step is forecasting the work and competencies of the future. Determining future work and competencies is foundational to assessing potential (promotability) because it takes time to develop talent and because future work and competencies may be different from those needed at present.

Chapter 5

Step 4: Forecasting the Work and Competencies of the Future

by *Frederick D. Loomis*

This chapter presents a methodology and framework to forecast an organization's future work and competencies (see Exhibit 5-1 on the following page). This chapter:

- Defines the term *strategic talent management forecasting*

- Explains the importance of a systematic planning process in the context of analyzing trends, developing scenarios and forecasting competences which will be needed for the future

- Provides a step-by-step model, with examples and tools to guide the process of ongoing strategic talent management forecasting, planning and evaluation

- Describes best practice models used by organizations in developing an effective strategic talent management forecasting system

Exhibit 5-1: The Step-by-Step Talent Management Model—Step 4

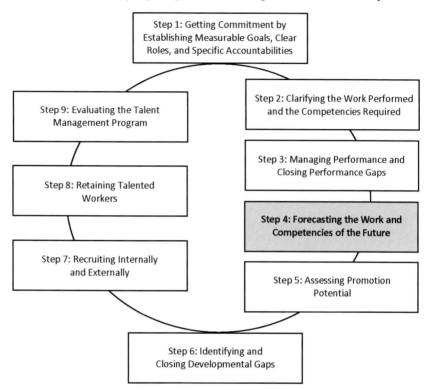

Defining Strategic Talent Management Forecasting

Strategic talent management forecasting refers to systematic efforts to anticipate future trends which will impact an organization's strategy with particular reference to new or strengthened competencies which will be needed for tomorrow's workforce. In this context, *strategic talent management* goes beyond identifying, developing and retaining productive and employable people. It includes a careful consideration of how work is performed now *and* forecasting how it might change in the future, in the context of an organization's vision and business strategy.

Looking to the Future: Key Global Talent Management Trends

Organizations should begin this process by asking a few simple questions: What do we think will happen in the future and what do we think this means for our organization? From past experience, we know that many trends will have an impact on the future workplace and talent management needs. This chapter begins with a discussion of key trends that have an impact on talent management. In addition to those discussed here, there are many others with will be unique to the context of specific organizations. Therefore, each organization needs to do an "environmental scan" to identify the key global and contextual trends which may impact the organization's strategic plan, with particular reference to talent management issues.

Among the trends discussed in this chapter are the following:

1. Economic uncertainty
2. Increasing globalization
3. Changing technology
4. Process and product innovation
5. Growing importance of intellectual capital and knowledge management

Trend 1: Economic Uncertainty. The ongoing global financial crises of the 21st century, which have occurred in various forms since 9/11, provide a dramatic demonstration of the risk inherent in any strategic plan that relies on a one-dimensional view of the economic future. Massive investments for wars in Afghanistan and Iraq, followed by rupture of the housing market, have choked the liquidity of the U.S. financial system and the crisis has spread across the world. Unexpected events can result in sharp revisions to economic forecasts, so organizations must be vigilant in monitoring leading indicators of change.

The corporate sector is often looking for government stability and leadership on the economy, so that they can develop corporate strategy with greater certainty. When there is a lack of government consensus about economic policy, organizations must be prepared to react to shifting economic scenarios, making long-term work-force planning very difficult. Strategic planning, particularly "scenario planning" tools, discussed later in this chapter, often provide very useful information for managing economic uncertainty (Schoemaker, 1995). The value of scenario planning is to help organizations better understand what might influence different plausible futures and to build a strategic thinking capability within the organization to identify which scenario is becoming most likely over time.

Trend 2: Increasing Globalization. The increase in global trade and the global marketplace is driving many organizations into the international economic arena. As a result the world economy has become more interconnected and interdependent. The Internet created the first real-time global data networks, unleashing a Tsunami of global information flows. Since then, more than 200 free-trade treaties have been signed and countries like China and India, after years of relative isolationism, are now more fully engaged in the global economy (Beinhocker and Stephenson, 2009).

As the market pushes firms into the globalized economy, organizations must adapt their strategic talent management policies. To support a global organization, an integrated strategy for talent management is needed. Competencies of global leaders must be identified and measured. Issues related to language, cultural diversity, learning styles and practices need to be considered in addressing this trend. From all indications, it appears that this trend will continue to be a critical issue as leaders and profession-als around the world develop new competencies to meet the chal-lenges of the global business environment.

Trend 3: Changing Technology. As noted in the globalization trend, the impact of the Internet and related technology-driven innovation has been profound. This trend has also created a grow-ing field of technology-based learning in the workplace. These technologies incorporate presentation, as well as delivery method and make use of interactive multi-media, videoconferencing, virtual reality, simulations, groupware, and electronic support systems. Online learning in university environments represents highest growth area for higher education. This trend has continued to workplace training and development. Employees today are extremely busy and cannot find the time to attend a formal place-based training session. This situation necessitates that more training be delivered at or near the work site, often in small increments to minimize disruption. Technology enhanced simulations which provide real-time feedback represent a promising trend in workplace learning.

Trend 4: Sustaining and Disruptive Innovation. Innovation and creativity are the hallmarks of business success. One need look no further than organizations like Apple, McDonald's and Disney. Through a series of product innovations, Apple changed the way we interact with electronic devices. McDonald's approach to fast food changed the restaurant business. Disney's unique characters and interactive theme park experiences changed the entertainment business.

A process innovation could involve something as small as improving efficiencies from modifying machinery or changing procedures. *Sustaining innovation* involves making something bigger and better. Examples include computers that process faster, cell phone batteries that last longer or cars with better gas mileage. In contrast, *disruptive innovation*, changes the bigger and better cycle by bringing to market a product or service that is *not* as good as the best traditional offerings but is more affordable and easier to use (Chistensen, 2011). Online learning is a good example. A computer-based lecture that you could consume anytime in your own home was considered to have higher value that a face-to-face class requiring a commute and a weekly schedule. Disruptive innovation often requires new and different competencies and therefore presents a significant challenge to strategic talent management planning.

Trend 5: Growing Importance of Intellectual Capital and Knowledge Management. Organization leaders are increasingly understanding the need to develop their intellectual capital and mange knowledge effectively. The intellectual capital of an organization represents the collective economic value of its workforce. Knowledge management is the effective use of intellectual capital (Rothwell, 2010). Both represent key assets for organizations which can be enhanced or diminished by the organization's strategy. Many organizations now use a combination of people and technology to manage their knowledge assets. Individuals provide an understanding of a given issue or context; technology can store and rapidly share this knowledge to further develop human capital. People in organizations possess important competencies (knowledge, skills and behaviors)—which can be developed and shared in a strategic talent management system. Simply stated, without people, no organization can function despite a growing reliance on technology to automate serving customers!

A Step-by-Step Strategic Model to Guide Implementation of a Talent Management Forecasting Program

Strategic talent management forecasting anticipates future trends which may impact an organization's strategy, with particular reference to new or strengthened competencies which will be needed for tomorrow's workforce.

The steps to the strategic talent management forecasting model include:

Step 1. Mission Clarification: *Who are we as an organization?*

Step 2. Strategic Trend Analysis: *What is happening in our environment?*

Step 3. Scenario Planning and Visioning: *How will these trends impact us? What kind of organization do we want to be in the future?*

Step 4. Competency Inventory: *What competencies currently exist within the organization?*

Step 5. Competency Needs: *In light of our vision and anticipated future scenarios, what competencies will be needed in the next 5-10 years?*

Step 6. Strategic Talent Management Forecast: *What is the gap between our existing competencies and our forecast of competency needs?*

Step 7. Strategic Talent Management Plan: *What is our future talent management strategy and what specific steps will we take to meet our future workforce needs?*

Each step of the strategic talent management forecasting model is presented in Exhibit 5-2, followed by a description of the process, useful tools, and examples.

Exhibit 5-2: Steps in a Talent Management Forecasting Program

Step 1. Mission Clarification: Who are we as an organization?

Yogi Berra, the famous New York Yankees baseball player and manager, once said, "If you don't know where you're heading, you're likely to end up somewhere else." Without a clear sense of purpose and values, organizations are lost. Therefore, missions provide meaning for an organization and its stakeholders.

The aim of mission clarification is to clearly specify purpose, philosophy, and values, so that everyone inside and outside the organization understands how you are, what you do and why you do it. Missions focus on useful and desired ends. Otherwise, organizations cannot hope to command the resources they need to survive, including committed stakeholders and loyal, high-performing employees.

Mission statements vary in length, but are usually short—not more than a page and typically can be summed up in just a few sentences and paragraphs. Formulating a mission statement should not be solely the work of the manager or executive. Adoption of a mission statement marks an important decision point in the strategic talent management forecasting and planning process. See the tool in Exhibit 5-3.

Exhibit 5-3: Tool for Mission Clarification

The development of a new mission statement or the clarification of an existing mission statement begins by posing key questions to key stakeholders of the organization:

- Who are we as an organization?
- Who are our customers, stakeholders or supporters?
- What business are we in?
- What social, economic, technological, or political issues or needs are we in business to address?
- How do we recognize, anticipate, or respond to these issues, needs, and challenges?
- What is our philosophy?
- What are our values?
- What makes us distinctive or unique?
- What are our core competencies as an organization and how does talent management system support the development of these competencies?

Example: Mission Statements

Academic Department of a Major Research University: To promote excellence, opportunity and leadership among professionals in the training and development field, including but not limited to those employed in business, education, government, and non-profit organizations.

Global Technology Company: We are committed to bringing the best personal computing experience to students, educators, creative professionals and consumers around the world through innovative hardware, software and Internet offerings.

Global Pharmaceutical Company: Our fundamental objective is to provide scientifically sound, high quality products and services to help heal, cure disease and improve the quality of life.

Step 2. Strategic Trend Analysis: What is happening in our environment? Examples of macro-level trends affecting talent management were discussed earlier in this chapter. This step of the model allows the organization to focus on those external trends and internal conditions that will potentially have the greatest impact on the strategic talent management forecast for the organization. The strategic trend analysis involves conducting an inventory of the political, economic, social, technological and market forces that can influence an organization's future strategy. The external trends can be identified through a systematic "environmental scanning" process, which examines research and published reports from experts in various fields (Bryson, 2004). Opportunities and threats in the environment are identified. Internal conditions are also categorized as strengths and weaknesses within the organizations. Simply creating lists of trends is not enough; the trends must be analyzed, discussed and compared.

Use the tools in Exhibits 5-4 and 5-5 to help you in doing strategic trend analysis.

Exhibit 5-4: Tool for Strategic Trend Analysis

A strategic trend analysis will produce a list of opportunities and threats that will be used for scenario planning and visioning for the organization (step 3 of the model).

The following categories and indicators can guide this analysis:

✓ **Political influences**: policies, laws and regulations affecting the business and workforce

✓ **Economy:** indicators that affect available and qualified labor pools, i.e., unemployment rates and housing prices

✓ **Social**: changing demographics and cultural influences

✓ **Technology**: changes that may impact products, services or talent management

✓ **Talent Management Pool**: changing composition of the workforce, outsourcing. turnover, enrollments in curricula needed to support new strategies

Exhibit 5-5: Sources of Data to Perform Trend Analysis

Society for Human Resource Management: www.shrm.org

U.S. Department of Commerce, Bureau of Economic Analysis: www.bea.gov

U.S. Department of Labor, Bureau of Labor Statistics (labor market forecasts): www.bls.gov

U.S. Department of Education, National Center for Education Statistics http://nces.ed.gov/

Example of Trend Analysis

A trend analysis can be summarized in a table which displays external opportunities and threats and internal strengths and weaknesses. An example of a SWOT analysis for Global Coffee Company is displayed in Exhibit 5-6.

Exhibit 5-6: Sample Trend Analysis (SWOT) for Global Coffee Company

STRENGTHS	WEAKNESSES
• Profitability ($800 million revenue) • Strong brand and reputation • Valued workforce • Strong ethics and values	• Declining innovation and creativity • Limited international portfolio • Dependent on coffee as main product line • High turnover rate; limited opportunities for advancement
OPPORTUNITIES	THREATS
• New products and services, such as Fair Trade products • Expand globally to India and Pacific Rim • Co-branding opportunities with other companies or causes	• Will market for coffee grow? • Rising cost of raw materials • Increased competition

Step 3. Scenario Planning and Visioning: How will these trends impact us? What kind of organization do we want to be in the future?

A *vision* is a statement of a realistic, credible, attractive future for an organization (Bryson, 2005). This model proposes that a vision grow out of a scenario planning process that flows logically from the strategic trend analysis performed in Step 2. By identifying trends and uncertainties, organizations can construct scenarios that can help to compensate for the typical limitations of traditional planning: over confidence and tunnel vision (Schoemaker, 1995). Scenario planning helps to make sense of data by constructing well-reasoned forecasts of what the future might hold generally, and specifically for the organization under study. See the tool to help you with scenario planning in Exhibit 5-7.

Exhibit 5-7: Tool for Scenario Planning and Visioning

Following are key elements of scenario planning and visioning (Schoemaker, 1995, Rothwell, 2010, and Bryson, 2005):

1. Define the scope of the scenario: set timeframe and scope of the analysis (products, markets, geographic areas and technologies)

2. Identify major stakeholders: customers, suppliers, share-holders, employees

3. Articulate key strategic issues from trend analysis and SWOT

4. List key uncertainties and threats

5. Construct scenario themes and validate with key stake-holders

6. Develop forecasting models on most likely scenarios (e.g., your informed "best guess of how the organization will be functioning in 5 – 10 years)

7. Write a narrative scenario that describes the organization's situation, competition, profitability and structure

8. Based on the scenarios, identified a preferred future and vision for the organization

A vision for an organization should be compelling and credible. It should encourage new products and services and build culture and values among its employees. Finally, a vision should identify the core human capital competencies that are needed for the future of the organization.

Example of Scenario Planning and Visioning for Human Resources

A team from Pricewaterhouse Coopers used scenario planning methods to forecast the organization of the future (Managing tomorrow's people: The future of work to 2020):

> Organizations operating in today's world are facing some of the greatest management challenges in the history of business: the talent crisis, an aging workforce, rising demands for global worker mobility as well as organizational and cultural issues emerging from the rapid pace of technological change. Research uncovered three major themes: 1) business models will change dramatically; 2) people management will present one of the greatest business challenges; 3) the role of human resources will undergo fundamental change. These themes suggest three possible future scenarios:

> *Corporate is king: the Blue World*:

> - Big company capitalism rules
> - Organizations continue to grow bigger
> - Individual preferences trump beliefs about social responsibility

> *Companies care: The Green World*:

> - Social responsibility dominates the corporate agenda
> - Concerns about demographic changes, climate and sustainability become the key business drivers

Small is beautiful: The Orange World:

- Companies begin to breakdown into collaborative networks of smaller organizations
- Specialization dominates the world economy

Source: Managing Tomorrow's People: The Future of Work to 2020
http://www.pwc.co.uk/eng/issues/managing_tomorrows_people_the_
future_of_work_to_2020.html

Step 4. Competency Inventory: What job competencies currently exist within the organization?

Competency identification is the most critical aspect of the Strategic talent management forecasting model. A *job competency* is defined as "an underlying characteristic of an employee (i.e., motive, trait, skills, aspects of one's self image, social role, or a body of knowledge) that results in effective and/or superior performance on in a job" (Rothwell, 2010, p. 82). A competency inventory is a process of discovering job competencies, particularly the competencies of "high performers" within departments and job categories. Businesses in the United States are estimated to be spending about $100 million per year in identifying competencies for their organizations (Rothwell, 2010). Competencies can be identified through self-assessments and structured interviews. Many technology-based systems are in use to support competency identification. However, competency software will not replace careful thought and analysis within the organization. See the tool in Exhibit 5-8.

Exhibit 5-8: Tool for Developing a Competency Inventory (Behavioral Event Interviews)

Rothwell (2010) has developed a qualitative approach to competency identification, using a structured protocol to conduct behavioral event interviews (BEI) with exemplary performers. Here the interviewer asks a series of detailed questions about actions performed in the work setting that employees perceive to be successful (or unsuccessful) and the thoughts, feelings and outcomes that accompanied them. Identifying competencies unique to exemplary performance is the goal of this approach. Typical behavioral event interview questions include:

1. What are your work requirements?

2. What was your most difficult or challenging assignment in doing this work?

3. Describe the assignment and situation in detail. When did it occur? Who was involved? What were you thinking and feeling as the events unfolded?

4. To what extent were you successful in meeting this challenge?

5. As you reflect on this incident and others like it, what personal attributes allowed you to be successful?

Step 5. Competency Needs: In light of our vision and anticipated future scenarios, what competencies will be needed in the next 5 to 10 years?

This step in the process involves forecasting the size of the workforce and specific job competencies which will be needed in the future based on the current inventory and the vision and likely future planning scenarios (steps 2-4). How is the organization positioning itself to meet future scenarios? What action steps can the organization take to meet the opportunities and threats identified in Step 2? How can the organization build on its strengths and address identified weaknesses? Strategic talent management forecasting is most likely to be successful when key trends are recognized and agreed to by management, and appropriate competency data is available to do the forecasting. See the tool in Exhibit 5-9.

Exhibit 5-9: Tool for Identifying Competency Needs

The following questions can guide the identification of competency needs:

1. Considering the trends and likely scenarios, indicate what functions and positions are most likely to be affected?

2. What is the most likely consequence of the scenario on this function/position?

3. How will the organization respond to future scenarios? What aspects of work must change? What structural changes are needed?

4. What new competencies (or positions) are required, given the scenarios and vision of the organization?

Step 6. Strategic Talent Management Forecast: What is the gap between our existing competencies and our forecast of competency needs?

As noted by Rothwell (2010), the use of competency models is one of the best ways to forecast future talent management needs. Organizational leaders are asked to review each key position to identify the competencies (motives, traits, skills, self-image, social roles and knowledge) which should, if future scenarios hold true, result in superior performance, consistent with the organization's vision. The resulting competency models are used as a guide to prepare individuals for advancement or to begin to recruit or develop new talent for the future.

Step 7. Strategic Talent Management Plan: What is our future talent management strategy and what specific steps will we take to meet our future workforce needs?

Best practice approaches to talent management are typically guided by a strategic model that helps human resource practitioners and strategists to more systematically integrate individual efforts into a cohesive plan. The result should be a shared vision for the organization, with the strategic talent management plan addressing the most critical future human capital needs. An exemplary strategic management plan will go beyond the identification of future competency models and will address issues such as how work is performed, the transfer of knowledge, and ethics and values in the workplace.

The strategic talent management plan must also have a strong evaluation component. Is it worth the costs? Is it meeting the organization's needs? Are there missing elements of the plan which must be addressed. Ideally, this evaluation should take place on an annual basis, with adjustments to scenarios and plans as necessary.

Finally, it is important to note that, for a strategic talent management plan to have credibility, it must have the full commitment and support of organizational leaders at every level. See the tool for preparing future-oriented competency models in Exhibit 5-10.

Exhibit 5-10: Tool for Preparing Future-Oriented Competency Models

An organization's vision and strategy can be vague to employees. Rothwell (2010) notes that a vision can be made clearer when plans are made job-specific. The tool below illustrates how a self-assessment can be used with each job incumbent to prepare an analysis and job-specific forecast for key positions. These worksheets can then be analyzed by organizational strategies, human resource professionals or external consultants to produce strategic talent management forecast.

Current Job Activities	How will these activities change in the future?	What new competencies are needed?

Best Practice Models

A 2009 report by the American Society for Training and Development (ASTD) identified several organizations as having exemplary practices in talent management. Best practice models for strategic talent management forecasting combine sophisticated planning models with methods for determining attrition rates, promotion rates, and other talent-related factors. A leading example of a company taking an even more comprehensive systems approach to talent management is Darden Restaurants. At Darden, a systemic framework addresses all facets of talent management for the organization: business strategy, culture, organization structure, objective alignment, and leadership behaviors.

Another best practice model identified by ASTD (2009) is Steelcase, is an international office furniture and office technology company. Steelcase established its talent management as a center of excellence and shared service with continuous support from global teams representing HR, IT, and Steelcase University. Steelcase developed a global human capital data bank that can gather and share information from a single data base system allowing the organization to leverage talent globally.

ASTD (2009) also noted the talent management model used by Computer Science Corporation (CSC) a global consulting, systems integration, and outsourcing company. CSC's approach to building a talent pool is focused on building enterprise-wide succession planning capabilities to identify future leaders early in their careers. CSC has implemented a standardized process, using a team approach and competency model to identify top-tier candidates for future leadership positions. This facilitates greater internal mobility and opportunities for rotational assignments. There is also a special track for women in leadership, as well as a diversity council.

Chapter Summary

This chapter addressed the efficacy of a strategic approach to fore-casting the work and competencies, which will be needed by organizations in the future. Information about future trends, organizational assessment, employee competencies and future work requirements is essential to an effective strategic talent man-agement forecast and plan. While information and a systematic process are important, leadership commitment and strategic analy-sis and action are the most critical variables in forecasting the workforce of the future.

Chapter 6

Step 5: Assessing Promotion Potential

by *Maureen C. Jones*

This chapter will provide a step-by-step approach to evaluating the promotion potential for your employees or candidates (see Exhibit 6-1 on the following page). The chapter will cover the following areas:

- Step One: Defining competencies for the position

- Step Two: Deciding who should be responsible for assessing potential promotions

- Step Three: Finding the best fit: Employee and job

- Step Four: Delineate the promotion potential assessment plan

- Step Five: Assessing potential: real-time approaches

Assessing individual promotion potential is a critical element in any talent management program. There is a need in a global market to consider what the internal pool of employees has to offer the organization for the next level up job. "Savvy companies understand the competitive value of talented people and spend considerable time identifying and recruiting high-caliber individuals wherever they can be found" (Bryan, 2006). Therefore, every company should develop a clear plan on how to assess the promotion potential of current employees and outside candidates. What is clear is that a rise in the number of applications for jobs means that there is an even greater need for assessment at all levels in an organization (Burbridge, 2008).

Exhibit 6-1: The Step-by-Step Talent Management Model—Step 5

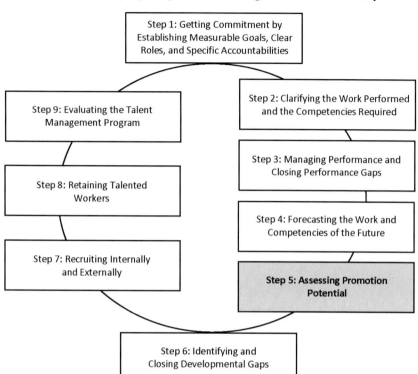

Understanding the talent within a company including strengths and weaknesses for each individual can set up a long term plan to identify, develop and then place employees in positions at least one level up from their current role. Has your company considered how they will decide which employee or candidate will have the potential to fill the next open position? Knowing which employees in the organization have the potential to fulfill higher level positions opens up many options. To assess how well the candidates are likely to perform if promoted, consider the following steps when developing your organization's promotion potential assessment program.

Step One. Clearly define the competencies needed for the position. Each position should require a specific set of competencies. Evaluating the competencies for each position and level on the organization chart assures a complete promotion potential assessment for each candidate. Making detailed job descriptions available for all employees will allow them to assess themselves for job fit and plan future needs. Putting the job specifics in writing reduces the appearance of favoritism and increases objectivity in the promotion process (Messmer, 2004). Helping employees to understand expectations can be essential to having employees ready to step up when openings occur.

Step Two. Who Should Be Responsible for Assessing Potential Promotions? Each candidate who is successful in performing his or her current job will need a complete assessment. However, it is important that the right person lead this process. The organization should decide who will be the best assessor for each position—or else appoint a coordinator for all promotion assessments. A good assessor will possess a range of skills but, in particular, must have excellent interpersonal skills. The assessor will need to coordinate all assessment activities, assimilate the collected data, and determine the proper ranking of candidates. The assessor will need to listen carefully, ask the right questions, obtain the level of detail required, build rapport quickly, and understand the organization's competency models to make accurate decisions. The organization also needs to be clear about the assessor's role, whether it is limited to gathering data only or also includes making recommendations or decisions about the promotion potential for each slate of candidates.

Step Three. Find the Best Fit: Employee and Job. Just like H_2O can exist as ice, water, and steam, work can be stratified into discreet levels (Carter, 2008). *Job fit* is an important focus as too often employers rely on past performance as the sole indicator for future performance. Excellent performance at the current position only provides some of the information needed. It is a common mistake to use it as the main assessment. Managers often assume that good at "this" means good at "that". Being a star performer in the current position may not be a permanent trait and does not equal readiness for promotion (Railway Gazzette, 2007). Additionally, the organization should create opportunities to evaluate potential abilities including one-to-one coaching up a level. This option pairs potential candidates with next level on-the-job experiences to evaluate fit.

Step Four. Delineate the Promotion Potential Assessment Plan. To assure your organization moves through the promotion potential assessment process smoothly, a plan need to be in place that clearly defines the roles of all involved. Whether it is a team of assessors or an individual, each assessment should flow easily form one step to the next. Creating a plan with an agenda, but which allows for flexibility to meet the specific needs of the candidate, the lead assessor should provide the following:

- Establish the short-term and long-term agenda

- Identify and communicate participant roles

- Define and communicate what criteria will be used to make the potential decision: pass/fail or remediate, provide resources and continue with the process

- Select approaches that will best evaluate "this" candidate (to be discussed in the next section)

Remediation can be an important approach for the employee and assessor/assessment because it will provide a clear plan that allows the employee to gain skills they do not currently possess. The remediation plan is created jointly by the assessor/manager and employee and identifies the area(s) for improvement with attainable goals. Each goal in the plan will have a date attached so that meeting objectives in a timely manner will keep the process on track. Having a written plan will also allow the management team to document when an employee does not make an effort or is unable to meet the job requirements.

Step Five. Assessing Potential: Real-Time Approaches. Possibly the most critical element of this process is assuring the right approach is used for the right situation. Many approaches are available. Each organization's leaders need to decide how and when each approach will be used. It will be important to decide on an approach and be sure the assessor knows how to implement the assessment approach effectively as well as evaluate its outcome. Many of the approaches listed below can be used together to form a global assessment of the individual. It is a widely held opinion that it is a mistake to use just one approach. A well-rounded assessment will include evaluating the candidate in several ways and making a decision with as much input as possible.

Manager nomination: The current or previous manager provides a detailed, written nomination for the employee. The report includes examples of how the employee currently meets/exceeds standards and how they would do the same for the next level up position. The manager uses the job description like a checklist and provides supporting data for each of the criteria.

360-degree assessment: A 360-degree evaluation considers all of the people and departments that any given employee would interact with during their current and/or future job duties and asks for input about the candidate's skills and abilities. This process can be done once or on an on-going basis for long-term evaluation. Each individual is provided with a competency evaluation. Obtaining feedback from many stakeholders will often allow discovery that may not be accessible to leadership. The stakeholder group may include other department managers, outside vendors, direct-report employees, support staff, customers, peers, and other interested stakeholders. See an example of a 360-degree tool in Exhibit 6-2 on the following page.

Exhibit 6-2: 360-Degree Assessment Tool

Directions: Please rate the employee in the following areas, providing specific examples whenever possible.

Communication skills: Communicating needs, expectations, new information/ideas; making sense of information

Decision-making abilities: When given the opportunity, do they take chances; decisive decision making; innovative; takes action; patient when called for

Organizational skills: Maintains organized processes/meetings/ plans/projects

Conflict management skills: Manages conflict and provides negation leadership

Interpersonal skills: Easily cultivates relationships with colleagues; adaptability; identifies potential and creates an environment of innovation; openness to influence; leadership; power

Internal abilities: Internal drive; coping mechanisms and ability to cope with multiple pressures; ability to self-assess; and current position and business knowledge

Note that most organizations conduct talent review meetings. Central to those meetings is typically a promotion assessment form for each High Potential Candidate. It is difficult to find examples of such forms, but see the example in Exhibit 6-3 on the following page. Feel free to modify it to meet your organization's needs. Of course, developing ratings on competencies for promotion requires relatively objective approaches. They are described below.

Assessment centers: The assessment center method involves multiple evaluation techniques, including various job-related simulations—and sometimes interviews and psychological tests. Typical techniques include: In-basket exercises, group discussions, simulations of interviews with "subordinates" or "clients", fact-finding exercises, analysis/decision-making problems, oral presentation exercises, and written communication exercises.

Realistic job tryouts: Employees assume, temporarily, a higher level job during a time when their manager is out of the office at a conference or on vacation (Rothwell, 2011). These opportunities allow a reality-based assessment of the employee's abilities and areas for improvement. As potential is identified, resources and training are provided. This method provides an accurate assessment on a level-up position unlike any other option.

Exhibit 6-3: Personal Potential Profile

PERSONAL POTENTIAL PROFILE

1. Name: _____ 2. Date of birth: _____

3. Nationality: _____ 4. Gender: ☐ M ☐ F

5. Current job/organizational level: _____

6. In current job since: _____

7. List previous jobs below:

Appointment	Dates	Jobs/Employer

8. Key organizational achievements:

- _____
- _____
- _____

9. Languages (F = Fluent, NF = Not fluent):

_____ ☐ F ☐ NF   _____ ☐ F ☐ NF

_____ ☐ F ☐ NF   _____ ☐ F ☐ NF

10. Competency Profile:
    O=Opportunity for Development; D=Developed; W=Well Developed

Foundational	O	D	W
Commitment			
Drive for results			
Embracing diversity			
Integrity			
Self-awareness and self-regulation			
Teamwork			

Exhibit 6-3 (continued)

Functional	O	D	W
Leading vision and change			
Strategic and global thinking			
Planning, setting standards, and monitoring work			
Managing resources			
Team leadership			
Coaching			
Networking			
Influencing			
Building trust			
Judgment			
Decisiveness			
Tact			
Communication			

Which, **if any,** are the 1 – 2 **OUTSTANDINGLY** developed competencies of the worker?

11. Profile of Technical Knowledge*—Requirements: Attachment No. 2

I. Technical Requirements for all Functional Areas	O	D	W
Professional work experience			
Knowledge of this organization			
Language			
II. Function—Specific Technical Requirement	O	D	W
Academic qualification and training			
Expertise			
Knowledge of this organization			

Exhibit 6-3 (concluded)

12. Overall performance from the Performance Management Form in the past 2 years (HE=Highly Effective; E=Effective; NE=Not Effective):			
1st Year (most recent)		**2nd Year (second recent)**	
❏ HE ❏ E ❏ NE		❏ HE ❏ E ❏ NE	

13. Suitability for representative positions (indicate level of worker for which the candidate is ready):		
Ready Now	**Ready in 1 – 2 Years**	**Not Ready**

14. Suitability for higher-level positions (indicate level/field for which the candidate is ready):		
Ready Now	**Ready in 1 – 2 Years**	**Not Ready**

15. Risk of loss to the organization:		
Risk Now	**Possible Risk in 1 – 2 Years**	**Not a Risk**

16. Individual career goals (if known):

17. General comments (if any):

Name: _____ Signature: _____ Date: _____

Step-up assignment: Assure all approaches are relevant to the job description being considered for this employee. Matching the job description with skills and abilities that will be assessed is a must for an accurate assessment. Additional assessment techniques may include:

- **Case study exercises:** Present the candidate with a variety of case studies that include prior and potential experiences to evaluate their decision making abilities, critical thinking, ability to adapt, leadership qualities and more. For example present a case in which a company that sells clothing to a wide variety of markets is having trouble with its customer service phone department. Customer service ratings have been dropping over the last four months. Ask candidates how they would tackle the situation. What steps would they take first, second and so forth?

- **Role play:** Give candidates an actual issue facing the organization to see what how they would respond. An alternate option is to give them real-life situations that have already occurred. This approach allows the assessor to determine if the candidate is capable of performing at the level required for the positions for which they are applying. For example present the candidate with the following role play:

  – The candidate plays the part of the executive and another person plays the part of an employee reporting fraud within the department.

  – The candidate is challenged to ask the right questions they would have to ask to determine problems and solutions as if they were already in the higher-level position. Watch how they respond to the employee, use interpersonal skills, and use resources.

Team experiences: Most leaders will need to work in a team environment and this method will provide an opportunity to evaluate their interactions on a team. The situation may be real-time or one created for the assessment. The candidate could take on multiple roles within the experience so the many skills may be assessed.

Problem solving exercises: During the assessment phase it is imperative to delineate the candidates' ability to solve problems they will likely face in the new positions. If there is an assessment team from various departments, each member could create examples pertinent to their area.

Some measures should be taken in this process to make it a positive experience. Proper assessment will avoid placing workers in positions for which they are ill-suited. As a part of the overall conclusion the assessor should provide constructive feedback that will allow candidates to use it to build future competencies. Keeping the organization's reputation in mind, the assessor should be sure candidates have adequate knowledge of the assessment process and should avoid surprises or experiences that do not lend themselves to learning.

Chapter Summary

Assessing promotion potential can be a rewarding and enlightening experience for both the organization and the candidate. A successful process includes defining competencies for the position, deciding who will complete the assessment and make decisions, finding the best fit for the employee with the job, delineating a plan and choosing the best assessment approaches. Each approach will lend itself to a specific job or candidate. Approaches may include: 360-degree assessments, manager nominations, realistic job tryouts, problem-solving, role-plays, team experiences, and case studies. The investment in a potential assessment plan will provide the organization with options for positions and information that can shape training and development.

Chapter 7

Step 6: Identifying and Closing Developmental Gaps

by *William J. Rothwell*

The sixth step is identifying and closing developmental gaps (see Exhibit 7-1). This step aligns individual competence with the profile of the ideal performer at the next higher level of responsibility. For instance, competency assessment reveals that an individual needs to build competence so as to be "ready now" for promotion. The sixth step closes this gap, preparing an individual to be "promotion ready."

Exhibit 7-1: The Step-by-Step Talent Management Model—Step 6.

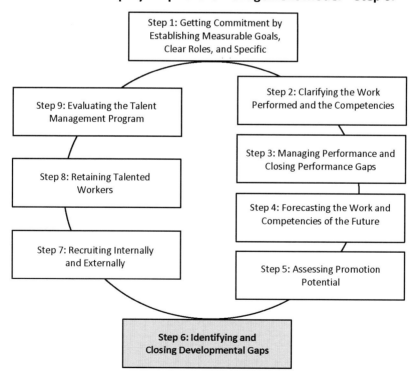

But what is a developmental gap? How does it differ from a performance gap? How can developmental gaps be identified? Once identified, how can developmental gaps be closed so that individuals are ready for promotion? How is individual development planning carried out, and what approaches can be used to close development gaps? This chapter answers these important questions.

Defining a Development Gap

A *development gap* is defined as the difference between the competencies that individuals possess and what they must possess to be promotable. Recall that competencies differ by level on the organization chart. For that reason, then, the competency profile of a front-line supervisor differs from that of a middle manager, and the competency profile of a middle manager differs from that of a top executive. Using potential assessment, described in the previous chapter, an organization's leaders may *objectively* determine what gaps exists between an individual's current competency profile and that required for promotion. Using objective approaches is superior to relying on more subjective views of "readiness" based on assumptions, which can always be prone to the "like me bias" or the "like us bias" (which refers to the tendency to hire people like ourselves or for a group to pick someone who is very much like them.)

Of course, development gaps may be understood in more than one way.

One kind of development gap is the difference between an individual's current competency profile and the minimum required for promotion. In short, what are the minimum competency differences that need to be closed so that an individual is promotable? That is the *minimum gap*.

A second kind of development gap is the difference between an individual's current competency profile and that required to match the profile of a fully-successful performer. A fully-successful performer is not the most productive job incumbent but is rather better understood to be the median or mean average performer. In short, what are the differences required to make an individual match that of an average performer at the next level up on the organization chart? That is the *average gap*.

A third kind of development gap is the difference between an individual's current competency profile and that required to match the profile of the organization's best-in-class performers. Recall that best-in-class performers may be as much as *20 times* more productive than average performers. They are the most productive performer. Achieving that gap will be exceptionally difficult—and perhaps impossible for some, since not all competencies may be developed and may have to be selected for. That is the *exemplary gap*, which takes its name from the best-in-class performers who may be called *exemplars*.

How Development Gaps Differ from Performance Gaps

Performance is usually understood to mean results—that is, out-puts and behaviors. A *performance gap* is the difference between an individual's present competency profile and that required to match the desired profile for that level on the organization chart. It also includes how well performers are getting results and how well they should be getting results to match expectations for that level on the organization chart.

A *performance gap* indicates that performers need to improve to match the profile for their existing levels on the organization chart. A *development gap* indicates that performers need to improve to match the profile for the next step up on the organiza-tion chart. By distinguishing these gaps, organizational leaders can avoid confusion over what is required to be promotable. It also helps to avoid the so-called *Peter Principle*, which is the (errone-ous) assumption that success at one level on the organization chart will absolutely guarantee success at the next higher level.

For the most part, performance gaps compare the individual to work requirements at present and at the individual's current level on the organization chart. Development gaps, on the other hand, compare the individual to work requirements in the future and at the next higher level on the organization chart. One reason that time should be considered is that it is usually impossible to prepare someone immediately for promotion. Developmental efforts take time.

How to Identify Development Gaps

There are many ways to identify development gaps. The previous chapter described some of them. The more precise, and objective, those development gaps can be pinpointed will make it easier to identify how to develop (or select) people for higher-level positions. For more information on how to pinpoint development gaps, see Rothwell, 2010.

Closing Development Gaps

Closing development gaps requires planning. It cannot happen immediately.

Popular approaches to closing development gaps adheres to the so-called *70-20-10 rule.*

Ten percent of development occurs through planned training, such as online and onsite. While training is often the first thing that managers think of when tasked to close development gaps, it is actually the least effective. After all, good training is expensive to design, develop and implement. Worse, only 8 percent of off-the-job training transfers back to the job in changed behavior.

Twenty percent of development occurs through social learning, mentoring, peer relationships, coaching and social networks. People can be developed through exposure to observing effective role models and imitating what they do, an idea associated with *social learning.* People can learn by pursuing informal teachers called mentors who have an unselfish regard for those they help and advise. Peer relationships can be effective in learning, since individuals can learn from their colleagues—such as on teams and in task forces. And social networks such as Twitter, Facebook, LinkedIn, and YouTube can be effective in connecting peers for learning in planned or unplanned communities of practice.

Seventy percent of development occurs through on-the-job learning. Work experience is prized precisely because people can learn from what they do and have done. They can learn by who they interact with, who they report to, and who their colleagues are. They can learn by what they do. They can learn by when or where they are required to perform. They can learn by why or how they perform. In short, *work experiences can be planned to build competencies.*

Individual Development Planning

An *Individual Development Plan* (IDP) is an action plan to narrow developmental gaps.

Two issues should be considered in individual development planning. One issue is the form to be used. The other issue is the process to be carried out.

The IDP Form

Many examples of IDP forms can be found on the web. But most forms include some typical elements. They include:

- The name of the person to be developed
- The name of the immediate supervisor
- The period of the planning process
- What competency gaps need to be addressed
- What actions should be taken to close the competency gaps (referring to the 70-20-10 rule)
- How the results will be evaluated
- What resources (time, money, staff) are needed to ensure that the development actions will be achieved

A sample IDP is shown in Exhibit 7-2.

Exhibit 7-2: a Sample Individual Development Form

Name:	Date:
Supervisor's Name:	Time Period for this IDP:

	PART I: DEVELOPMENT NEEDS
1	In the space below, describe what competencies the individual should develop. Refer to any assessment results previously completed.

	PART II: ACTION PLAN
2	Describe how the individual should build the competencies referenced in #1 above. Consider articles or books to read, training to attend or participate in, work experiences or work assignments, people who would be good mentors, and any other ideas on how to build competence. Specify the time by which the development activities should be completed. Continue on an additional sheet of paper, if needed.

Exhibit 7-2 (concluded)

PART III: EVALUATION

3	For each developmental action listed in #2 above, indicate how it will be evaluated. Continue on an additional sheet of paper, if necessary.

PART IV: RESOURCES

4	For each developmental action listed in #2 above, indicate the time, money, and resources available to complete it. Continue on an additional sheet of paper, if needed.

PART V: APPROVALS

Signature of Supervisor:	Signature of Worker:
Date:	Date:

The IDP Process

The IDP process is typically performed annually on individuals who are deemed promotable. IDPs can (of course) be done for all employees. But one philosophy of talent management is that developmental investments are best made in people who are both good performers and are also considered promotable because they are most likely to lead to a superior return on investment.

The IDP process should begin with the supervisor, since individuals "do not know what they do not know to be developed for promotion." Hence, supervisors should identify the developmental gaps (using the objective approaches described in the previous chapter) and then decide how best to meet them. Some organizations make information available on a Learning Management System (LMS) to guide developmental planning. For each competency and behavioral indicator that an individual needs to develop, the LMS may list a large number of possible resources that could be used to build competencies. Examples of resources might include:

- Articles to read
- Books to read
- Videotapes to watch
- Audiotapes to listen to
- Websites to visit
- Onsite courses sponsored by the organization
- Offsite courses sponsored by other organizations
- Coaching tips on how to build competence from those who are good at it
- People inside the organization to tap as mentors who are good at the competency
- Work assignments that will build competency
- Places where the competency is demonstrated best
- Other resources that may be helpful in building competencies

Using this information, an individual's supervisor prepares an initial draft of the IDP and then meets with the individual to review the suggestions. This meeting should be more upbeat than a performance review, which employees may sometimes confuse it with. But the goal is to focus on the positive—that is, the future and development—rather than past or present performance. A supervisor's goal is typically to motivate the worker to develop and to ensure that sufficient time, money and other resources are made available to help implement the IDP.

Chapter Summary

This chapter answered several important questions:

- What is a developmental gap?

- How does it differ from a performance gap?

- How can developmental gaps be identified?

- Once they are identified, how can they be "closed" so that the individual is ready for promotion?

- How is individual development planning carried out, and what approaches can be used to close development gaps?

The next chapter focuses on recruitment, which can be an alternative to development. Instead of building competencies inside the organization, another option is to recruit someone from inside or outside the organization. Integrating recruitment and development is particularly important in talent management.

Chapter 8

Step 7: Recruiting Internally and Externally

by *Maria T. Kirby*

This chapter offers a step-by-step approach to recruiting the right talent, both from inside and outside the organization (see Exhibit 8-1 on the following page). This chapter:

- Explains the difference between "Replacement Planning" and "Talent Management" approaches

- Details the steps for both internal and external recruiting

- Details the policy considerations for both internal and external recruiting

- Outlines the creation of talent pools within the organization

- Offers strategies for maximizing applications from high-quality talent when recruiting externally, and

- Provides strategies for integrating internal and external recruiting efforts

Exhibit 8-1: The Step-by-Step Talent Management Model—Step 7

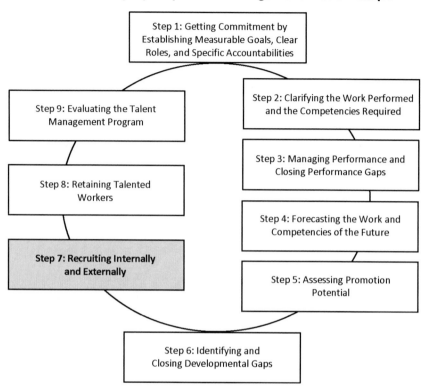

Replacement Planning versus Talent Management

There is an important distinction to be made between just replacing individuals as they exit an organization and talent management. In fact, talent management has little to do with reactive, transactional 'replacing', and has everything to do with planning, cultivating and maintaining talent pools—both inside and outside the organization.

Although it is common to think of the management and executive staff when developing a recruiting strategy as part of talent management, recruiting strategy should encompass all levels of the organization. Consider all the areas within the organization where rare or technical knowledge is held. How do you maintain this workforce, and how do you staff first-line supervisors who must possess both management skills and technical knowledge? Does your organization have high turnover in some entry-level positions? What is the cost (in out-of-pocket expenses and lost productivity and customer service) lost through this workforce churn?

Simply replacing staff as they exit puts the organization in a reactive position, making it difficult to be strategic because hiring is taking place within the context of a deficit. Even at the executive level, where there is more likely to be notice of exit and planning for new staffing need, the organization should have a recruiting strategy that is sophisticated enough to identify and translate the long-term talent needs of the business into performance needs that will inform recruiting decisions—including whether new talent should be developed internally or sourced externally.

Successful Recruiting Requires Cultivation

Recruiting is both an art and a science that requires planning and regular attention, regardless of an organization's current hiring needs. An organization which has consistently cultivated both its internal staff and its external reputation (sometimes called its *employment brand*) will have more talent options available to it when job openings do become available. Conversely, if an organization fails to develop its own talent or reputation in the external labor market, it could find itself struggling to source quality applicants when vacancies do arise. Recruiting should not be done only when vacancies exist but should be a continuing process, driven by a strategy.

Both internal and external recruiting methods prompt considerations which offer some guidance as to which strategy should be employed. Recruiting internally is a preferred approach within many organizations for developing supervisory and management talent, as promoting internally helps to ensure that candidates are a good fit within the organization's culture, which is a major consideration with regard to retention. The professional references and performance records of internal hires can be much more thoroughly and reliably evaluated, and in highly-technical fields it may be most efficient and effective to train staff with existing technical expertise in new skill areas, like supervision and management.

Additionally, internal hiring that spans different levels and departments of an organization may help to build connections within the company based on the knowledge and relationships that new hires carry with them into their new role.

There are costs associated with internal recruitment strategies, however, including the expenses associated with recruiting, hiring and training a replacement for the vacancy a candidate leaves in the wake of their move. Other considerations exist in addition to cost, including the double-edge sword of employee morale, as consistently hiring externally may be demotivating for staff members who value the availability of career/promotion opportunities within the organization. However, any perception of unfairness or favoritism in internal hiring practices can be equally harmful to morale, so internal hiring policies and criteria must be fair and transparent.

Recruiting externally also has costs and benefits that dictate when it is the most advisable strategy. For example, when there is a need for an organization to adapt a dramatically new way of operating, it may be most efficient and effective to onboard an external hire who is not mired in the insulated thinking of one organization's provincial way of doing things. The same is true when new hires must begin their new roles with objectivity and not be influenced by existing social networks within the organization. In some cases, external recruiting may also be recommended when roles are temporary, involve leading a group of peers through a significant change process, or when the necessary skills do not exist and cannot be easily developed from the existing workforce.

Cost considerations specific to external recruiting include the obvious cost of attracting, interviewing and orienting new staff, as well as increased risk of on boarding an individual with an unproven track record. Cultural fit is also a consideration, as individuals who do not successfully assimilate into an organization's culture have a much higher risk of turnover than individuals who have already accepted and adapted to organizational behavior and norms. Even well-planned and executed recruiting efforts are costly, and organizations are advised to consider retention to maximize the efficiency of recruiting spend.

Determining and Implementing Recruiting Strategy

Most organizations use some combination of internal and external recruitment. However, the outcome of efforts will be maximized when there is a guiding strategy in place. Drivers of strategy include considerations of the availability of necessary skills inside and outside the organization, workplace culture and the specific demands of the vacancy.

Step 1: Determine Your Recruitment Strategy.

Consider Internal Recruitment

- How technical and/or rare are the skills that will be needed by the hire? If the skills required are either rare in the external labor market, or highly-technical and related to core-competencies of the organization, consider developing internal talent and recruiting internally

- How much demand is there for talent in your industry? If fierce competition exists for top talent, consider promoting staff development and career advancement opportunities and trying to develop and retain promising staff. The opportunity for advancement within the organization may promote a culture of staff loyalty

Consider External Recruitment

- Are the skills required by the vacancy very new or different than what currently exists in the talent base? Or does your organization want to start doing things in a distinctly new/different way? If so, consider recruiting external talent with skills and experience in-line with the established need

- Will the new hire have to exercise great objectivity with regard to staff and/or organization decisions? Consider recruiting externally so that the successful candidate arrives to their duties without an existing social network or clique of favorite coworkers

- Does the job require leadership of a significant change effort among a group of peers? If so, consider recruiting a new team member who will represent a fresh start and will not be handicapped in the change effort by a perception from peers of being a part of the old way of doing things

Step 2: Plan Ahead. The right time to establish an approach to recruiting is actually long before the organization needs to fill a vacancy. Both internal and external recruiting approaches require planning in order to be successful—internal recruiting requires a targeted employee training and development program, and external recruitment requires that the organization cultivate a positive reputation in the labor market. An organization suffering from high employee turnover or with a reputation for poor management, inadequate compensation, undesirable working conditions, employment instability or unfair employment practices will likely to have a difficult time recruiting quality talent. Organizations must take stock of these considerations, make any necessary adjustments, and promote the positive attributes of their workplace. Bear in mind that every current (and former!) employee of your organization can influence the organization's reputation as an employer, so care should be taken to maintain positive and fair impressions with staff.

If an organization elects to pursue an internal recruitment strategy, the development of 'talent pools' is one approach based in the principles of talent management through which to cultivate internal talent. The fundamental concept is simple; multiple individuals across units, departments and levels of the organization are developed to enable lateral or horizontal moves on the organization's career ladder (Rothwell, 2011). This is in contrast to traditional replacement planning, where perhaps one individual would be targeted and groomed to replace (usually) a key management or executive role. Instead, organizations that invest in developing talent pools will have multiple individuals who have continually been acquiring the training necessary to move into areas of need when they arise.

Step 3: Establish and Enforce Recruitment Policies. Once the organization has determined its overall recruiting strategy and begun the planning process to support it, clear guiding policies should be developed and shared openly with staff at all levels. Recruitment policies are important for many reasons, and especially to protect internal recruits from any fear of retribution from current supervisors who may learn of new employment bids, as well as to help protect morale when coveted positions are filled by new hires, rather than by a candidate from within.

At minimum, internal recruitment policies should address:

- Any consideration that will (*or will not*) be given for seniority

- An emphasis of the freedom of current employees to bid on opportunities for which they are qualified, without fear of retribution from current supervisors
- How postings are to be promoted internally, including how, where, and when they will be posted

- Established guidelines for staff transitions, including the length of notice required and the handling of salary increases (or decreases) for moves (down, up or laterally) within the company

- Establishment of minimum qualifications, including whether or not there is a formula by which years of experience will equate educational attainment

- Length-of-service requirements (especially for jobs that require major corporate investment or staff relocation)

- Maximizing career ladders for talented workers while minimizing job-hopping from those seeking small salary gains or escape from a personality mismatch with coworkers:

  - Supervisors must be coached not to good references to 'good riddance' employees as a means to pass them off to another part of the organization

  - Be clear about minimum qualifications (especially education and experience) so that employees do not become discouraged by apply for and being passed over for jobs they are not qualified for

- Establish clear expectations related to transitions so that candidates do not leave projects unfinished or otherwise "disconnect" from existing position while in pursuit of another opportunity

Likewise, external recruiting policies should be in place to help an organization grow its talent base when it cannot be sourced internally when, for example, the speed of growth is too great to develop and backfill position, or when the workforce lacks the necessary competency base. Having clear policies in place can help an organization avoid some of the most common pitfalls of external recruiting.

At minimum, external recruitment policies should address:

- Whether or not internal candidates will be given first option at job openings (and whether or not every posting should be advertised both internally to maximize the potential for talented applicants)

- What materials are required as part of an application, both in terms of standard items like cover letters and references, as well as potentially deal-breaking details like salary requirements

- Establishment of logistical details, like hours of operation, telecommuting options and any other potential workplace flexibilities (in large and professional organizations these types of considerations are usually best handled via policy, rather than by individual or ad hoc consideration).

- Regular cultivation of the organization's 'employer brand' and regular maintenance of talent pipelines (example: job fairs, university graduates, etc.)

- The alignment of workforce pipelines with career ladders and other employment factors like the competitiveness of compensation (For example, public organizations may consider focusing on recent college graduates who may be more willing to accept lower pay in exchange for career experience than seasoned industry professionals)

Utilizing these policies may help an organization avoid common pitfalls associated with external recruiting, including:

- Lack of working knowledge of the new individual

- Risk of culture miss-fit

- Some channels for recruiting (i.e.; Internet job sites) are designed to result in more passive applications/applicants

Maximizing Applications from the External Talent Pool

An organization which is able to attract a large pool of applicants is more likely to be able to find the best and most appropriate talent for their staffing need. With this in mind, note that external recruiting requires good marketing and development of the organization's reputation as a desirable place to work. Incentives like tuition reimbursement, flexible work schedules, career opportunities, a desirable work environment and competitive compensation plan help to define an organization as an employer of choice, facilitating the attraction of the most desirable talent.

Also consider your approach to connecting with talented. Employee referral programs are a very good way to source potential applicants, as current staff will usually provide some level of screening before they recommend a candidate. Existing workers have knowledge of the corporate culture and job requirements, which ideally will aid them in referring candidates that will be a good organizational fit. As a follow-on benefit, the referred candidate may feel an obligation to live up to the referring employee's recommendation, leading new hires to hold themselves to a higher standard. Over time, a well-managed employee referral program may also result in a sort of organic quality management culture where staff members have a vested interest in their collective success.

Organizations are also advised to keep track of where the best employees have come from and cultivate recruiting opportunities there. Sources may include universities, job fairs, related industries or organizations and/or from links within the supply chain who may represent the best culture fit or bring with them valuable industry knowledge and experience.

Steps to Integrate Internal and External Recruitment

The right mix of internal sourcing versus new hires will vary by organization and be based on a variety of factors, including size, competency base, size of employment need, and availability of talent (both internally and externally). Consider the following strategies and steps to effectively integrating internal and external recruitment:

Step 1: Evaluate Needs and Plan Ahead. Start by evaluating the business need. How quickly is the organization growing? What is the turnover rate? Are there any major changes anticipated that will necessitate new skill sets? What percentage of the workforce has an interest in working their way up in the organization and would therefore take on the necessary training and development? How available is talent in the external market?

As you evaluate your organization's responses to these questions, consider the areas and functions of the organization where you wish to maintain the status quo, as well as the areas and functions that would benefit from change and a fresh start. If your organization has a stable, moderate growth rate and the existing workforce is willing to engage in developing their capabilities, then consider establishing a leadership development program for a majority of your promotions. Utilizing internal hires will further stabilize the organization's culture, which is fine so long as that is the objective.

The areas which are showing rapid growth, managed change or cultural dysfunction are the most likely areas to target for external recruitment. In cases of rapid growth, an internal training and development schedule just may not be feasible due to the size of the employment need and the speed with which skilled individuals must be in place. In this case, it is advisable to hire external talent. In the case of change or organization culture issues, it is likely advisable to seek an external candidate who can both represent and champion change without being mired in 'the way things were' or caught up in relationships with peers who are resistant to change and/or are the cultivators of cultural dysfunction.

It must be emphasized, however, that if there are competencies which must be developed before internal staff will be suitable for recruitment, integrating recruiting approaches will require investment into planning, training and time.

Step 2: Align the Recruiting Strategy with the Organization's Strategy. Consider the organization's strategic plan and business objectives and plan the recruiting approach with guidance from the policy and purpose questions presented earlier in this chapter. Take into consideration any plans for change, major growth, or significant change in strategic direction, and examine the plan for any new core competencies that must be developed. Remember that training and development of internal recruits will require time and planning. The organization's strategy should reflect the investment into training and development as well as investment into employee incentives that will help to build the organization's employer brand.

Step 3: Implement a System to Track Potential Retirements, Turnovers and Promotions. If it is not already being done, organize a system to predict and track retirements and succession (promotions). Be strategic about preparing for predictable turnovers, allocating sufficient time for internal training and development or external employer brand development and recruiting—especially for significant employment needs.

Step 4: Implement the Necessary Internal Development Mechanisms and Attend to the Cultivation of the Organization's Employment Brand. It may be difficult for a peer in a unit to be promoted into a position of authority and gain the respect and authority necessary from those who had recently been peers. To be successful with internal recruiting, an organization is advised to make the path to promotion very clear so that promotions cannot be viewed as 'popularity contests' or otherwise invoke undue jealousy. Rather, lay out the path to promotion with development and service milestones that both groom potential leaders and help them establish credibility within the organization even before they assume a leadership position. It is also important to establish expectations relevant to any consideration that will be granted for seniority, although note that seniority alone is NOT a recognized qualification for promotion within the context of talent management. A well-defined management development program is one way to manage long-range internal recruiting and avoid many morale issues.

Use the tool in Exhibit 8-2 to help organize your thinking about recruitment.

Exhibit 8-2: A Tool to Guide Decision-Making for Internal and External Recruiting

SKILLS/ COMPETENCIES	IF "YES," THEN →	RECRUITING STRATEGY	POLICY CONSIDERATIONS	RECOMMENDATIONS
Does the job require rare or technical skills that exist within the company, but are hard to find externally?	⬆	Recruit internally and develop the skills necessary in the new role.	Have clear policies in place with regard to consideration granted to seniority, minimum education required, etc.	An internal Leadership Development Program may help develop leadership competencies in technical staff, and give them management credibility in the eyes of their peers.
Will this position need to lead a significant change effort?	⬆	Recruit externally and hire an individual with a fresh perspective who has the necessary competencies to lead change but is free of ties to old ways of doing things.	Enact a policy that both external and internal recruiting efforts will be utilized so as to maximize the opportunity of attracting the best candidate (help manage expectations and morale when external recruiting is desirable).	Track and cultivate connections with the best sources of external talent (i.e., university recruiting events, industry job fairs, etc.).

Exhibit 8-2 (concluded)

SKILLS/ COMPETENCIES	IF "YES," THEN →	RECRUITING STRATEGY	POLICY CONSIDERATIONS	RECOMMENDATIONS
Does this position require complete objectivity with regard to existing workforce?	⬆	Recruit externally and hire an individual who is free from relationships/ biases with existing staff.	When objectivity is key, provide appropriate training for incoming hire and ensure that any orientation process does not convey any unwanted bias.	Where personnel management is a large component of a role, ensure hiring decisions focus on management and supervisory skill rather than technical background, per se.
Is this role a natural progression from existing staff's roles?	⬆	Focus recruiting efforts internally to provide an opportunity for advancement to an existing employee.	Establish guidelines with regard to any required tenure in positions, confidentiality of applications, and internal recommendations from supervisors to prevent conflict over internal bidding.	Coach management staff such that they support qualified staff in seeking internal opportunities for advancement.

Chapter Summary

This chapter discussed the importance of internal and external recruitment in talent management. Obviously, there are really only two ways to source talent—that is, develop it internally or recruit it internally and externally. A different chapter examined development; this chapter examined internal and external recruitment. This chapter explained the difference between replacement planning and talent management approaches, detailed the steps for both internal and external recruiting, detailed policy considerations for both internal and external recruiting, outlined the creation of talent pools within the organization, offered strategies for maximizing applications from high-quality talent when recruiting externally, and provided strategies for integrating internal and external recruiting efforts.

Chapter 9

Step 8: Retaining Talented Workers

by *Maria T. Kirby*

This chapter reviews the steps to retain talented workers. This chapter:

- Explores common reasons for turnover

- Explores the notable consequences of turnover (cost!!!)

- Provides a step-by-step strategic model to guide implementation of a retention strategy

- Describes what potential issues organizations should be aware of when implementing retention strategies

See Exhibit 9-1 on the following page.

Exploring Common Reasons for Turnover

As you consider investments in recruiting, hiring and training the best available talent, bear in mind that skilled workers nearly always have many employment options. Even if your workers are not actively looking for other jobs, they may be recruited by competitors, so it is wise to implement a retention strategy as part of comprehensive talent management efforts to secure the investments your organization has made in recruiting, selecting and developing its workforce.

Exhibit 9-1: The Step-by-Step Talent Management Model—Step 8

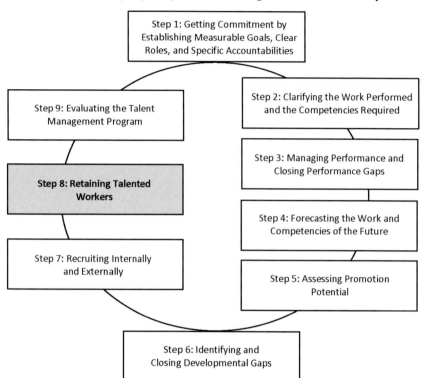

Loss off workforce is generally known as *turnover*. It can be costly. Estimates of the costs of turnover vary. But one calculation suggests that it may cost as much as $3,500 to replace an employee earning $8 per hour. Other sources estimate the cost of turnover at 30–50 percent of the worker's annual salary (see http://www.cba. org/cba/practicelink/mf/overhead. aspx). Temporary firm Manpower estimated in January 2011 that 84 percent of U.S. workers planned to quit their jobs in 2011 (See http://money.cnn.com/ 2010/12/23/ pf/workers_ want_new_jobs/index.htm.)

Although many reasons explain why employees voluntarily separate from an organization, three of the more common catalysts include:

- Management/personnel issues
- Job and compensation issues
- Personal issues

Strategically managing these issues can serve as the foundation of a systematic retention program. That can help an organization safeguard its workforce investments and ensure a continuity of projects, goals, customer service and stability of organizational culture. The first step to managing for turnover is to understand common underlying causes.

Management and Personnel Issues

Problems with supervisors and coworkers are a very common complaint. A talented employee with other employment options may take advantage of opportunities to escape personality conflicts or frustrating management practices. Ineffective leaders may lack in interpersonal or communication skills, be unapproachable, or allow personal issues to affect their ability to work closely with and supervise their colleagues. Additionally, inconsistencies in how workers are treated and evaluated may be very frustrating. Bad management practices can lead to feelings of annoyance and insecurity. So it is important that those in supervisory positions are chosen for their management skills and not just promoted into a leadership role because of their technical expertise in previous positions.

Job and Compensation Issues

Job-related frustrations are also common and may be related to goals and metrics which are under-developed or unclear, leading staff to feel frustrated as they try to meet job demands. Frustration may also be prevalent in workers who are under resourced, demoralized by working conditions, or subject to rigid policies that take away a workers sense of control over their employment situation.

Even with apt supervision, job and/or compensation factors may also affect an organization's ability to retain workers. It is important not to undervalue the best talent, because most workers are well aware of what their employment value is in the job market. Unless there are other factors at play to retain them, even small pay differentials may be sufficient to lure top staff members away. Also consider how you are utilizing your best talent. There are many theories that can be considered with regard to engaging employees' skills. The most comprehensive of them emphasize the importance of providing variety in tasks and taking care not to promote good staff beyond their capacity.

Personal Issues and Positive Turnover

On the subject of turnover and retention, it is also worth noting that some churn is both positive and, at times, inevitable. Employees with outdated and irrelevant skills should be either retrained or allowed to exit the organization. Industries have an average rate of turnover for specific positions. If an organization experiences churn at or below the industry average, it may be benefiting to some degree from new perspectives as workers in an industry often move between competitors and even up and down the supply chain. Likewise, some turnover is simply inevitable due to life events, family or health issues. So it is wise to take this into consideration when developing talent management and succession plans.

Cost Considerations of Retaining Talent

Understanding the common causes of turnover is only the first piece of the equation. It is also critical that organizations understand all of the costs that are associated not only with recruiting and training new workers (a cost which, in some industries, can be equal to as much as half or more of the annual salary of that position), but also with regard to productivity, employee morale and customer satisfaction. Not only do new employees often take months to acclimate and truly become productive in their new role and environment, but constant churn of staff may result in discontinuity with regard to company goals, projects or even corporate culture. Retaining talent is especially important in high-touch industries where the front-line staff is a part of the product experience for the customer, such as the front line teller staff in the banking industry. It is likewise important to employee morale that they do not experience constant churn in coworkers to such a degree that they feel dispensable or unstable in their positions.

Many root causes can lead to turnover, and organizational efforts to address turnover require comprehensive solutions (see Rothwell, 2007). Use the tool in Exhibit 9-2 to help you organize your thinking about turnover.

Exhibit 9-2: Common Causes of Turnover

PERSONNEL ISSUES	
Potential Cost	**Suggested Remediation**
• Voluntary turnover • Disruption of teamwork • Low morale • Quality and workflow problems	• Hire managers with good interpersonal skills • Provide training in supervisory skills • Provide teamwork training and development for staff
JOB AND COMPENSATION ISSUES	
Potential Cost	**Suggested Remediation**
• Voluntary turnover • Frustrated or resentful staff • Low morale • Production shortfalls • Quality issues	• Remediate any substandard workplace conditions • Achieve industry parity for compensation and benefits • Strive for alignment between workforce skill and interest and assigned role and duty

Exhibit 9-2: Common Causes of Turnover (continued)

PERSONAL, HEALTH, AND OTHER	
Potential Cost	**Suggested Remediation**
• Voluntary turnover • Employment gaps if organization is not prepared	• While these issues may not necessarily be able to be remediated, human resource planning must be sufficient to produce a nimble response to employment gap

Step-by-Step Approach to Employee Retention

Retention programs can take various forms, depending on the professional characteristics of the employees, the expectations of workforce within the industry, and the ferocity of competition for talent in the labor market. A comprehensive talent management strategy must take all of these things into account. However; there are some fundamental steps that should be considered across most industries and organizations:

Step 1: Hire and train competent managers and supervisors.

Reduce Conflict and Personnel Issues through Employee Development

Hire management staff with consideration to their supervisory and interpersonal skills (in addition to more technical qualifications). A finer point but worth noting is that managing talented workers requires a supervisor who is not intimidated by someone potentially smarter or more talented than they are! Seek to hire and develop staff with a team mentality.

Step 2: Take steps to make sure staff know what is expected of them.

Establish Clear Performance and Behavior Standards and Resource Accordingly

Train staff in the specifics of their role so that they are clear on what the major points of evaluation will be in terms of output, quality, cycle-time and acceptable levels of waste. Integrate business literacy training into all levels of workforce development, such that workers have a working knowledge of the organization's competitive strategy and how their role impacts the success of that strategy, as well as how their role intersects with the roles of coworkers.

Provide hassle-free access to the resources that staff need to do their job efficiently and effectively. It is a very frustrating contradiction to have production expectations which are not matched with the necessary manpower, tools, materials or time.

Step 3: Empower workers.

Disperse Relevant Authority and Cultivate Feelings of Control over Employment Destiny

Empowering employees can include inviting their relevant feedback on work processes and procedures, granting them appropriate decision-making authority, and actively engaging them in problem-solving efforts. Organizations will gain efficiency and improved customer service when issues can be handled quickly, and staff will benefit from an increased sense of control within their work life.

Be transparent with information related to the health and status of the organization. Truly empowered employees should have access to as much relevant information as possible, especially with regard to potential layoffs or downsizing. Bear in mind that people will often assume the worst if they are not given information.

Step 4: Provide fair compensation and competitive benefits.
Benchmark competitors' pay and take stock of what the living standards are of the workforce you intend to hire and retain. In most cases, full-time workers should be receiving at least a living wage and mid-career professionals should be able to sustain a family.

In addition to fair monetary compensation, identify what motivates employees in your workplace and offer reasonable incentives and benefits flex time and appropriate positive recognition.

Step 5: Develop internal career paths for talented workers.
Provide Advancement Internal to the Organization

Talented workers are likely to be on the lookout for opportunities to keep their career progressing. Creating career ladders which provide advancement opportunities within the company may help organizations hold on to their best workers who may otherwise be lost to external employment options.

With regard to promoting within the organization, it is important to develop clear policies which promote fair workplace practices. Reward hard work and productivity—not popularity!

Also, be mindful of employee skill and motivation when restructuring positions and/or transferring staff. It is good to offer advancement and new opportunities, but roles and duties that may seem similar at a surface glance may be different enough to cause a talented employee to lose interest or perform poorly. The best operational staff may not enjoy or strategic work, and vice versa. Allow as much self-selection as possible to prevent miss-matches of skills and interests.

Considerations for Rolling Out a Retention Strategy

Manage for "good" turnover of poor performers and outdated skill sets. The goal of a good retention program is not necessarily to retain every single employee. Rather, the goal should be to develop and retain the best and most relevant talent within the context of a comprehensive Talent Management strategy. It worthwhile to direct efforts into getting talented individuals into roles which best fit them, but there will be some staff who are just not a good fit for the organization or even the industry. Construct internal development and career advancement opportunities such that investments are made into the staff which demonstrate the most potential to contribute to the organization's competitive strategy. You may accomplish this through selective hiring practices, screenings and leadership development programs which help to target training investments, and incorporating performance evaluation into the routine management function.

A comprehensive talent management strategy will support retention efforts. A good retention strategy is part of an overall Talent Management program that spans the spectrum from recruiting, selecting and developing the best talent. When care is taken at every step of the employment process to make good hires and invest in training the best workers, retention efforts can be very targeted to the specific needs of key talent. A retention program should not stand alone, however, as turnover due to inappropriate hires or poor investments into training are sunk costs and are not best addressed by reducing turnover.

Retention does require investment, but the returns are significant. Retention and other Talent Management efforts do come at a cost. However, the alternative of not investing into the workforce can be far more costly in terms of inappropriate hires, inefficiency in production, loss of customer satisfaction, and investment of training funds into poorly suited workers. Investing those same dollars into a Talent Management strategy to support appropriate hiring, development and retention adds value, whereas continual remediation of workforce churn is an expense which can be the most significant non-value-adding expense encountered by an organization.

Use the tool in Exhibit 9-3 on the following page to help you organize your thinking about how to integrate retention-oriented thinking in a Human Resource Management program.

Chapter Summary

This chapter reviewed the steps to retain talented workers. It explored common reasons for turnover, explored the notable consequences of turnover, provided a step-by-step strategic model to guide implementation of a retention strategy, and described what potential issues organizations should be aware of when implementing retention strategies.

Exhibit 9-3: Integrating a Retention Program into an Existing Human Resource Management Framework

STEPS	COMPONENTS
Step 1: Provide supervisory skills training to management staff	• Leadership Development • Planning and Organizing • Communication
Step 2: Clarify expectations of staff	• Train workers in the organization's competitive strategy • Cultivate business literacy, such that employees know how their role contributes to overall success
Step 3: Empower the workforce	• Distribute appropriate decision-making authority (i.e., allow discretion in customer service issues up to $100 level) • Provide regular communications on business issues
Step 4: Benchmark compensation and evaluate benefits	• Establish competitive compensation and benefits packages • Recognize and reward exemplary performance
Step 5: Develop Internal Career Paths for workers	• Establish job levels that reward professional development and achievement • Promote from within, when appropriate

Chapter 10

Step 9: Evaluating the Talent Management Program

by *William J. Rothwell*

Evaluating the program is the ninth and final step in step-by-step talent management (see Exhibit 10-1 below). This step answers a deceptively simple question: *how well has the talent management program worked?* While this step may focus on individual program components, it more typically examines the overall impact of the talent management program.

Exhibit 10-1: The Step-by-Step Talent Management Model—Step 9

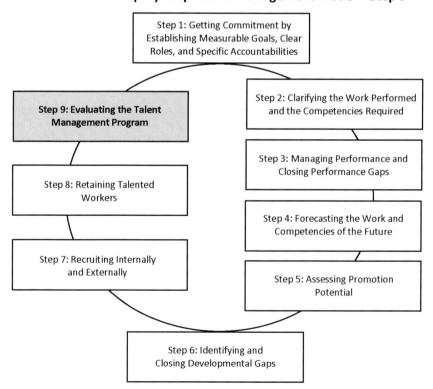

But what is meant by evaluating the talent management program? What should be examined in an evaluation, and how should it be examined? What metrics are commonly used in talent management evaluation? What step-by-step approach can guide talent management evaluation? This chapter answers these questions.

The Meaning of Evaluating the Talent Management Program

While inexperienced practitioners may think that evaluation is an activity that occurs only after a change effort, the reality is that evaluation can occur before, during and after. The same principle applies to evaluating a talent management program. *Talent management evaluation* determines how well the talent management program met the measurable goals established for the program and, in turn, how well those goals helped the organization achieve its strategic goals.

Evaluation is important because it demonstrates the value of the talent management effort (Rothwell & Kim, 2005). Additionally, evaluation allows for corrective action when program activities depart from program goals. In short, evaluation makes sure that the program remains aligned with program goals.

What and How Should Talent Management Programs Be Evaluated?

Some people—often that would include skeptical CEOs—may ask "what is the return on the investment in talent management programs"? The answer is simple: nobody knows. Nobody has calculated it. And, more to the point, nobody really cares, either. Why? The reason is that talent management programs are undertaken for specific business reasons—such as preparing the organization for pending retirements of leaders, challenging high potential workers, improving employee retention, staffing up to fuel the talent needed for company growth, or helping the organization change its strategic direction in the wake of mergers, acquisitions, takeovers, or other dramatic transformations. How well talent management program results match these goals should be the proper focus of evaluation, not necessarily the costs versus the benefits.

By implication, if the talent management program goals are unclear, then measuring its value will also be difficult. Say, for instance, that a major talent management goal is to "prepare sufficient people to be promotion ready to deal with an expected loss of 6 key executives to retirement." In this example, "preparing people to deal with the expected loss of 6 key executives" is a measurable goal. At the end of the year, decision-makers can compare the goal to the program results. By doing that, it can be seen if the program is operating successfully.

The lack of evaluation criteria can indicate that leaders were never clear, or in agreement, on what they wanted from the program. That is actually a common problem to have. To avoid it, coordinators of talent programs—such as HR managers—should make sure that the CEO and other senior executives have prioritized exactly what measurable results they want from the program. The coordinator can then supply information regularly to leaders about how well program results match program goals.

Common Metrics Used in Talent Management Evaluation

Several metrics are common in talent management. That is not to say that these must always be used. Again, the best metrics are tied to legitimate business needs and to program goals.

One common metric is the so-called *time to fill metric*. It refers to the lead time it takes to fill a position from the date it is approved to be filled until the first day that the successful candidate begins the position. The shorter the time to fill, the more successful is a talent program.

For some positions—such as CEO or a senior executive—the lead time could be quite long if no talent program is in place. One reason it takes so long is that the risk in making a bad decision is great. Consequently, organizational decision-makers—such as a board of directors—will take their time to source the best person for the CEO position rather than pick the first person who applies. A second reason is that senior jobs may require more decision-makers in making a decision. If an entire board of directors is involved in recruiting and selecting the best candidate, the speed of the decision hinges on the availability of the decision-makers. That can slow down the process.

There are hidden costs in long lead times to make decisions. If the organization lacks a CEO, it is a good bet that it will lack strategic direction while the top decision-maker is being decided upon. And the same principle applies for a division head or department head. Human nature being what it is, workers will usually avoid risky (and therefore innovative) actions while they have no supervisor to approve of what they do or to protect them from powerful leaders who might not share enthusiasm for their ideas. Consequently, and significantly, empty jobs at the top of the organization chart can lead to revenue loss.

But the time to fill metric is not adequate by itself to measure the success of a talent management program. Another metric to consider is the percentage of internal promotions to external hires. No organization wants to promote 100 percent from within for the simple reason that it will lead to insulated (some call it incestuous) thinking. Fresh ideas usually come from those who have no stake in the past. Decision-makers should set targets at the beginning of the talent management program for the percent of internal promotions to external hires. The more stable the competitive environment, the higher the percentage of internal promotions that are possible. For that reason, it is a common rule of thumb in government to promote 80 percent from within but hire 20 percent from outside at all levels. In contrast, organizations in the most competitive environments (such as high tech firms like Siemens, Motorola, Microsoft or Intel) are well-advised to target 20 percent to be promoted from within and 80 percent to be hired from outside. The reason: high percentages of external hires will lead to the most innovative thinking in tough, fast competitive environments.

Another important evaluation metric is critical turnover, defined as the percentage of high potentials that voluntarily leave the organization. While *regular turnover* focuses on the departures of all employees, *critical turnover* focuses on the percentage of promotable workers who resign over the total number of promotable workers. Obviously, if the organization is losing more promotable people than it is average (but not promotable) people, then it is losing valuable talent. That is much like a person who is bleeding internally. It marks a dangerous but hidden condition that must be uncovered and addressed before it damages organizational effectiveness.

Several other metrics are worth mentioning. One is the *percentage of workers who are retirement eligible*. That can be determined easily by asking the payroll department to run a report for the whole organization on the number of people who are eligible to retire. When that percentage is examined, it is best to present results in rolling three year periods (such as 2012, 2013, and 2014) because trends can be spotted more easily in these time segments. The payroll department can then be asked to go beyond the organization and to drill down by job code, level on the organization chart, department and facility. The result of this process should uncover that some places in the organization are, or will be, at higher risk of problems due to pending retirements than other places. That can provide valuable clues about where to pilot test a talent management program.

Yet another metric to examine is the *average time in various jobs*. How long have people been with the organization and in their jobs? People do not feel challenged if they are doing the same jobs for more than 5 to 7 years. These should be found and then actions taken to challenge people.

Many other metrics can be used to evaluate talent management. Some can be found on various websites. A simple web search for "metrics used in talent management" can uncover many such websites. One good place to look: the former Saratoga Institute, now owned by Pwc (see http://www.pwc. com/gx/en/research-insights/talent.jhtml) and http://greatworkplace.wordpress.com/2010/10/13/20-common-hr-metrics-their-formulas/.

A Step-by-Step Approach to Talent Management Evaluation

Step 1: Plan the evaluation by writing objectives to guide the evaluation process. The first step is to develop a plan for the evaluation. It is necessary to have a project plan that will guide the evaluation project so that it economizes resources. A plan is also a way to attract attention for evaluation among decision-makers, perhaps helping to recalibrate the goals of the program. After all, talent management program goals can (and usually should) change over time to take into account changing conditions.

One important point to remember in this step is to clarify the form that the final deliverable should take. In other words, how should the evaluation results best be presented and to whom? What stakeholder groups most want the evaluation results, and what will they do with those results? It is important to clarify the answers to these questions to ensure that the evaluation results yield information useful to stakeholders and will inform their future decisions.

Step 2: Decide what, when, who and how to measure. As part of the evaluation plan, be sure to clarify what information (data) should be collected, when it should be collected, who should lead the evaluation effort (and be on any evaluation team), and how the measurement will be carried out. For instance, should data be collected from various stakeholders (such as senior managers, HR managers, HiPos, or others)? Should evaluation be conducted before the talent management program is launched so as to forecast the benefits versus the costs of the program investment, at milestones during annual implementation, and at the end of each year? Should evaluation be carried out by HR practitioners, line managers, a team, consultants, or others? Should evaluation be carried out with secondary data, surveys, interviews, focus groups, or other methods (or some combination of them)?

Step 3: Collect information relevant to the evaluation. This step is nothing more than implementation of the project plan for talent management evaluation. But managing this step brings with it all the challenges common to any project management. That includes carrying out the project on a timely basis on or under budget.

Step 4: Analyze results. If the results are collected as numbers, they can be analyzed using quantitative methods. If the results are collected as words, they can be analyzed using qualitative methods. If the evaluation results take the form of both numbers and words, then both quantitative and qualitative methods must be used to collect data.

Step 5: Present results to key stakeholders. The results of the evaluation process may be presented in writing (such as a report) or in one or several oral presentations. The presentation itself will focus attention on the results achieved from the talent management program, serving to demonstrate its value. It will also give stakeholders a chance to rethink program goals so as to keep the program on target under changing conditions.

Step 6: Make improvements to the Talent Management Program based on the evaluation results. Evaluation can inform program improvements. To make best use of evaluation, decision-makers should be presented with evaluation results. The coordinators of the talent management program can use the results to guide a conversation with decision-makers about what to do to make continuing improvements to the talent management program.

Chapter Summary

This chapter defined *talent management evaluation* as the process of determining how well the talent management program met the measurable goals established for the program and, in turn, how well those goals helped the organization achieve its strategic goals. Many metrics may be used to measure the talent management program. But among the most popular metrics are the so-called *time to fill metric,* the *percentage of internal promotions to external hires,* and *critical turnover.* The key steps in evaluating a talent management program are: (1) plan the evaluation by writing objectives to guide the evaluation process; (2) decide what, when, who and how to measure; (3) collect information relevant to the evaluation; (4) analyze results; (5) present results to key stakeholders; and (6) make improvements to the talent management program based on the evaluation results.

Appendix

A Worksheet to Guide Development of a Proposal for a Step-by-Step Approach to Implementing Talent Management

Directions: Use the form on the following page to help guide you in the process of establishing a proposal for implementing talent management in your organization using the step-by-step approach described in this book. For each step under Column 1 below, indicate under Column 2 below what action you plan to take in your own organization, when you plan to take it, who will be responsible for the action, and how you will measure the results. Submit the final proposal to your organization's leaders for approval. Add paper to this worksheet, as necessary.

COLUMN 1	COLUMN 2
Steps in implementing Talent Management	**What action you plan to take in your own organization, when you plan to take it, who will be responsible for the action, and how you will measure the results.**
1. Getting commitment and establishing measurable goals, clear roles, and specific accountabilities	
2. Clarifying the work performed and the competencies required	

COLUMN 1	COLUMN 2
Steps in implementing Talent Management	**What action you plan to take in your own organization, when you plan to take it, who will be responsible for the action, and how you will measure the results.**
3. Managing performance and closing performance gaps	
4. Forecasting the work and competencies of the future	

COLUMN 1	COLUMN 2
Steps in implementing Talent Management	**What action you plan to take in your own organization, when you plan to take it, who will be responsible for the action, and how you will measure the results.**
5. Assessing promotion potential	
6. Identifying and closing developmental gaps	

COLUMN 1	COLUMN 2
Steps in implementing Talent Management	**What action you plan to take in your own organization, when you plan to take it, who will be responsible for the action, and how you will measure the results.**
7. Recruiting internally and externally	
8. Retaining talented workers	

COLUMN 1	COLUMN 2
Steps in implementing Talent Management	**What action you plan to take in your own organization, when you plan to take it, who will be responsible for the action, and how you will measure the results.**
9. Evaluating the Talent Management Program	

Notes

Chapter 1

Dubois, D., & Rothwell, W. (2000). *The competency toolkit.* 2 vols. Amherst, MA: HRD Press.

Dubois, D., and Rothwell, W. (2004). *Competency-based human resource management.* Palo Alto, CA: Davies-Black Publishing.

Rothwell, W. (2009). *The manager's guide to maximizing employee potential: Quick and easy strategies to develop talent every day.* New York: Amacom.

Rothwell, W. (2007). Organization retention assessment. In E. Beich (Ed.), *The 2007 Pfeiffer annual: Consulting* (pp. 177–188). San Francisco: Pfeiffer.

Rothwell, W., Jackson, R., Knight, S., Lindholm, J. with Wang, W., & Payne, T. (2005). *Career planning and succession management: Developing your organization's talent—for today and tomorrow.* Westport, CT: Greenwood Press/an imprint of Praeger.

Rothwell, W., & Kazanas, H. (1999). *Developing in-house leadership and management development programs: Their creation, management, and continuous improvement.* Westport, CT: Greenwood Publishing.

Rothwell, W., Sterns, H., Spokus, D., and Reaser, J. (2008). *Working longer: New strategies for managing, training, and retaining older employees.* New York: Amacom.

Chapter 2

Rothwell, W., & Kazanas, H. (2003). *The strategic development of talent.* Amherst, MA: Human Resource Development Press.

Chapter 3

Dubois, D., & Rothwell, W. (2000). *The competency toolkit.* 2 vols. Amherst, MA: HRD Press.

Prien, E., Goodstein, L., Goodstein, J., & Gamble, L., Jr. (2009). *A practical guide to job analysis.* San Francisco: Pfeiffer.

Sanghi, S. (2007). *The handbook of competency mapping: Understanding, designing and implementing competency models in organizations.* 2nd ed. Thousand Oaks, CA: Sage.

Chapter 4

Aquinis, H. (2008). *Performance management.* 2nd ed. Englewood Cliffs, NJ: Prentice-Hall.

Cokins, G. (2009). *Performance management: Integrating strategy execution, methodologies, risk, and analytics.* New York: Wiley.

Parmenter, D. (2010). *Key performance indicators (kpi): Developing, implementing, and using winning KPIs.* 2nd ed. New York: Wiley.

Chapter 5

American Society for Training and Development (ASTD). (2009). *The new face of talent management.* Alexandria, VA: Publications Department.

Ashton, Chris and Morton, Lynne. (2005). Managing talent for competitive advantage. *Strategic HR Review.* 4(5), 28–31.

Bryson, John M. (2004). *Strategic planning for public and nonprofit organizations.* 3rd ed. San Francisco: Jossey-Bass.

Christensen, Clayton M. (2011). *The innovative university.* San Francisco: Jossey-Bass.

Loomis, Frederick D. (2004). "Strategic Business Planning for Workforce Development." In *Linking training to performance: A guide for workforce development professionals.* Rothwell William J., Gerity, Patrick E. and Gaertner, Elaine A. (Eds.). Washington D.C.: American Community College Press.

PricewaterhouseCoopers. *Managing tomorrow's people: The future of work to 2020.* Retrieved from http://www. pwc.co.uk/ eng/issues/managing_tomorrows_people the_future_of_ work_to_2020.html

Robinson, M. et al. (2007) Forecasting future competency requirements: A three-phase methodology. *Personnel Review, 36*(1), 65–90.

Rothwell, W. (2010). *Effective succession planning: Ensuring leadership continuity and building talent from within.* 4th ed. New York: American Management Association.

Schoemaker, Paul J. (1995). Scenario planning: A tool for strategic thinking. *Sloan Management Review, 36*(2), 25–40.

Sumardi, Wardah A. and Othman, Rozhan. (2009). The three faces of talent management in Malaysia. *International Journal of Business Research, 10*(1), 181–185.

Chapter 6

Anonymous (2006). Promoting from within. *Risk Management, 53*(8), 8.

Anonymous, (2007, October 30). How to? Spot high-potential employees. *Railway Gazette.*

Burbridge, M. (2008). Assessing potential. *Training Journal, 39,* 39–42. Retrieved from http://search.proquest.com/docview/ 202954716?accountid=13158

Byham, W. C. (2004). What is an assessment center? Retrieved from: http://www.assessmentcenters.org/pdf/Assessment CenterArticle.pdf

Carter, M. (2008). Requisite organization design: A work levels approach. Retrieved from http://www.missionminded management.com/requisite-organization-design-a-work-levels-approach

Hu, J. J. (2008). The law of requisite cognitive capacity in human communication. *E:CO, 10*(4), 28–37

Lowell, B. L., Joyce, C. I. and Weiss, L. M. (2006). Making a market in talent. *McKinsey Quarterly*. Retrieved from: http://www.mckinseyquarterly.com/Making_a_market_in_talent_1765

Messmer, M. (2004). Recognizing potential starts by promoting from within. *Strategic Finance, 86*(4), 9–10.

Plemmons, P. (2009). Conducting an Internal Search. *Trustee, 63*(3), 26.

Rothwell, W. J. (2011). *Invaluable knowledge: Securing your company's technical expertise.* New York: AMACOM.

Studer, Q. (2006). Selecting and retaining talent: Tools for the bottom line. *Healthcare Financial Management, 60*, 7.

Chapter 7

Rothwell, W. (2010). *Effective succession planning: Ensuring leadership continuity and building talent from within.* 4th ed. New York, NY: American Management Association.

Chapter 8

Rothwell, W. (2010). *Effective succession planning: Ensuring leadership continuity and building talent from within.* 4th ed. New York, NY: American Management Association.

Chapter 9

Rothwell, W. (2007). Organization retention assessment. In E. Beich (Ed.), *The 2007 Pfeiffer annual: Consulting* (pp. 177–188). San Francisco: Pfeiffer.

Chapter 10

Rothwell, W., and Kim, Y. (2005). How are succession planning and management programs evaluated? In V. V. Ramani (Ed.), *Succession planning: Insights and experiences* (pp. 118–125). Hyderabad, India: ICFAI University Press.

About the Authors

 **William J. Rothwell, Ph.D., SPHR** is Professor of Learning and Performance in the Workforce Education and Development program, Department of Learning and Performance Systems, at The Pennsylvania State University, University Park campus. In that capacity, he heads up a top-ranked graduate program in learning and performance. He has authored, co-authored, edited, or co-edited 300 books, book chapters, and articles—including over 70 books. He is also President of his own consulting firm, Rothwell & Associates, Inc. (see www. rothwell-associates. com.)

Before arriving at Penn State in 1993, he had 20 years of work experience as a Training Director in government and in business. He has also worked as a consultant for more than 40 multinational corporations—including Motorola, General Motors, Ford, and many others. In 2004, he earned the Graduate Faculty Teaching Award at Pennsylvania State University, a single award given to the best graduate faculty member on the 23 campuses of the Penn State system. His train-the-trainer programs have won global awards for excellence from Motorola University and from Linkage Inc. His recent books include the edited three-volume *Encyclopedia of Human Resource Management* (Pfeiffer, 2012), *Lean But Agile: Rethink Workforce Planning and Gain a True Competitive Advantage* (AMACOM, 2012), *Invaluable Knowledge* (AMACOM, 2011), *Competency-based Training Basics* (ASTD Press, 2010), *Effective Succession Planning*, 4th ed. (AMACOM, 2010), *Practicing Organization Development*, 3rd ed. (Pfeiffer, 2009), the *Manager's Guide to Maximizing Employee Potential* (AMACOM, 2009), *Basics of Adult Learning* (ASTD, 2009), *HR Transformation* (Davies-Black, 2008) and *Working Longer* (Amacom, 2008). He can be reached by e-mail at wjr9@psu.edu.

Maureen C. Jones has been working in the health care field for more than two decades. She has Bachelors of Science and Masters of Science degrees in Nursing and has worked in some of the most challenging health care environments in the world. Through her work in inner-city emergency departments, and rural community hospitals, she has built a unique perspective on the assessment of talent in academic and business situations. Now a full-time member of the faculty of Penn State's School of Nursing, she utilizes her vast experience base to help prepare the nursing leaders of the next generation. She has over 20 years of assessing and evaluating talent for a variety of institutions. Maureen is a PhD candidate in Penn State University's College of Education, Workforce Education and Development, focusing on the selection, development and transitions of leadership in the health care industry.

Maria T. Kirby, MBA, has in-depth field experience from wide-variety of industries and has led companies in workforce development, business, infrastructure and capital development, and industrial and energy efficiency initiatives. Her professional experience includes economic development work with 130+ companies and multiple industry consortium groups. Kirby is currently the Director of the Business Program Portfolio for Penn State's Academic Outreach unit and she is enrolled in PhD coursework in Workforce Education and Development (Human Resource Development/ Organization Development track) in Penn State's College of Education (candidacy exams January 2012).

Frederick D. Loomis received his Ph.D. in higher education from Penn State University and currently serves as Assistant Clinical Professor and Director of the master's degree program in higher education at Drexel University. He has over 30 years of leadership experience in the higher education and public sectors, holding administrative appointments as dean, special assistant to the provost, executive director, and state-wide program director. With expertise in leadership, strategic planning, diversity, e-learning, competency modeling and workforce development, Loomis has held faculty and administrative appointments at Penn State University and Neumann University. He has consulted with state and local governments, school districts, career and technical centers, and higher education institutions in the United States, Egypt, and Tanzania.

Two Ends of a Leash

Unshackled

GRACE D. NAPIER

Published by Wheatmark™
610 East Delano Street, Suite 104, Tucson, Arizona 85705 U.S.A.
www.wheatmark.com

Publisher's Cataloging-In-Publication Data
(Prepared by The Donohue Group, Inc.)

Napier, Grace D.
  Two ends of a leash : unshackled / by Grace D. Napier.

  p. ; cm.

  ISBN: 978-1-58736-959-9

1. Blind women—Fiction. 2. Blindness—Fiction. 3. Blindness—Psychological aspects—Fiction. 4. Blindness—Social aspects—Fiction. 5. Social interaction—Fiction. 6. Blindness—Public opinion—Fiction. I. Title.

PS3614.A657 T96 2008
813/.6   2007936457